Business
Res

D0497321

Skills for Business Studies

Upper-intermediate

Louis Rogers

OXFORD

UNIVERSITY PRESS

Contents

Study focus

1 What do you think helps people form an opinion of another person? Think of examples in pairs.

nationality, clothes, voice, behaviour, …?

2 How might your country of origin or your cultural background affect your opinion? Think about:

- alcohol
- religion
- the roles of men and women
- other (what?)

3 Discuss your ideas in pairs.

Reading strategies

A | Predicting content

1 You are going to read an extract from an academic textbook about organizational behaviour. Look at the heading. What do you think the text might be about?

2 Look at three pictures from the same chapter of the textbook. What can you see in each picture?

Figure 1.1

Figure 1.2

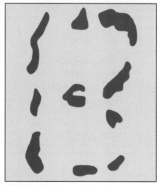

Figure 1.3

3 How do you think the three pictures in 2 are related to the text?

4 Read the text and check your predictions.

B | Reading closely for detailed information

1 Read the text again. Answer the questions about each paragraph.

A How do we understand the world around us? How do other people understand how we see the world?

B What do we do with information we receive about the world around us?

C In what way are language and culture connected?

D How and why might a South East Asian student upset a librarian?

E What is the difference in communication style between the UK, the USA and France?

2 Read the reactions to the manager's email in more detail (para. B, 1–4). Answer the questions.

a Which team leader may be happy to provide the information but be worried why the manager wants it?

b Which team leader may be hoping for more employees in their department?

c Which team leader may be worried about losing authority in their department?

d Which team member may be hoping to cut costs?

3 Which reaction would be similar to your own and why? Discuss in pairs.

C | Reacting to the text

How is your culture different from another? Think of an example. Explain how your example relates to the ideas in the text.

Glossary

mental (line 1): (adj) in the mind
dynamic (line 18): (adj) moving, changing
provokes (line 51): (v) causes
proficient (line 63): (adj) good (at sthg)
innocently (line 82): (adv) without meaning to
ambiguity (line 98): (n) having more than one meaning

Perception and communications

A Perception is the mental function of giving significance to stimuli such as shapes, colours, movement, tastes, sounds, touch, smells, pain, pressures and feelings. Perceived reality is the key to understanding behaviour.
5 How we perceive others and ourselves is at the root of our actions and intentions. Understanding the perceptual process can help develop insights about ourselves and may help in reading other people. The words we use, the way we look and the body language
10 we display communicate our view of the world. The importance of perception and communications in guiding our behaviour needs to be understood for effective relationships with others.

The Perceptual Process

B The significance of individual differences is particularly
15 apparent when focusing on the process of perception. We all see things in a different way. We all have our own, unique picture or image of how we see the 'real' world and this is a complex and dynamic process. We do not passively receive information from the world;
20 we analyse and judge it. We may place significance on information and regard other information as worthless; and we may be influenced by our expectations so that we 'see' what we expect to see or 'hear' what we expect to hear. Although general theories of perception were
25 first proposed during the last century, the importance of understanding the perceptual process is arguably even more significant today. Perception is the root of all organisational behaviour; any situation can be analysed in terms of perception. Consider, for instance,
30 the following situation: a member of the management team has sent an email to team leaders asking them to provide statistics of overtime worked in their section during the past six months, and projections for the next six months. Mixed reactions could result:

35 1 One team leader may see it as a reasonable request which will help lead to improved staffing levels.

2 Another team leader may see it as an unreasonable demand, intended only to enable management to exercise closer supervision and control over the
40 activities of the section.

3 A third team leader may have no objection to providing the information but be suspicious that it may lead to possible intrusion into the running of the section.

45 4 A fourth team leader may see it as a positive action by management to investigate ways of reducing costs and improving efficiency.

Each of the section heads perceives the email communication differently based on their own
50 experiences. Their perceived reality and understanding of the situation provokes differing reactions. So, despite the fact that a group of people may 'physically see' the same thing, they each have their own version of what is seen – their perceived view of reality. Consider
55 for example the image shown in Figure 1.1. What do you see? Do you see a young, attractive, well-dressed woman? Or do you see an older, poor woman? Or can you now see both? And who can say with any certainty that there is just the one 'correct' answer?

The Importance of Language and Culture

C Our language plays an important role in the way we perceive the world. Our language not only labels the environment for us but it also structures and guides our thinking patterns. Even if we are proficient skiers, we do not have many words we can use to describe
65 the texture of snow; we would be reliant on using adjectives. The Inuit, however, have 13 words for snow in their language. Our language is part of the culture we experience and learn to take for granted. Culture differences are relevant because they emphasise the
70 influence of social learning on the perception of people and their surroundings.

D So language not only reflects our experience but it also shapes whether and what we experience. It influences our relationships with others and with the environment.
75 Consider a situation where a student is using a library in a UK university for the first time. The student is from South East Asia, where the word 'please' is incorporated in the verb and in intonation; a separate word is not used. When the student requests help,
80 the assistant may consider the student rude because they did not use the word 'please'. By causing offence the student has quite innocently affected the library assistant's perceptions.

E Much is communicated in how words are said and
85 in the silences between words. In the UK, speech is suggestive and idiomatic speech is quite common:
'make no bones about it' (means 'get to the point')
'sent to Coventry' (means 'be socially isolated').
And action is implied rather than always stated:
90 'I hope you won't mind if' (means 'I am going to')
'I'm afraid I really can't see my way to …' (means 'no')

The ways in which words are used and assumptions made about shared understanding are dependent upon an individual's culture and upbringing. In
95 cultures where it is 'normal' to explain all details clearly, explicitly and directly (such as the USA), other cultures may find the 'spelling out' of all the details unnecessary and embarrassing. In France, ambiguity and subtlety are expected and much is communicated
100 by what is not said.

Source: LJ Mullins, *Management and Organisational Behaviour*, Pearson, Harlow 2007, pp.209–214

Business vocabulary

A | Noun collocations

Noun collocations are common in academic writing, partly because more information can be packed into a shorter sentence.

1 Which sentence in each pair do you think is more likely to be in an academic text?

  a 1 Effective relationships in the workplace are key to a successful working environment.

      2 Relationships that are effective in the workplace are key to a successful working environment.

  b 1 The team responsible for management met to develop a clear strategy.

      2 The management team met to develop a clear strategy.

  c 1 Developing methods for reducing costs on a project is key to profitability.

      2 Developing methods which reduce the costs on a project is key to profitability.

2 <u>Underline</u> the phrases in 1a–c that are more academic. Circle the equivalent phrase in the other sentence.

3 Match the type of noun collocation to the example in *italics* in sentences a–c.

  noun + noun   verb + noun   adjective + noun

  a The importance of perception and communications in guiding our behaviour needs to be understood for *effective relationships* with others.

  b A member of the *management team* has sent an email to team leaders.

  c A fourth team leader may see it as a positive reaction by management to investigate ways of *reducing costs*.

4 Rewrite sentences a–d using noun collocation patterns. Compare in pairs.

> The manager wanted to improve the levels of staffing.
> *The manager wanted improved levels of staffing.*

  a The differences between individuals affect how we perceive the world.

  b The leader of the team had little impact on the project's success.

  c The company must address the needs of the markets that it targets.

  d We work well with our clients because we share an understanding of what we want to achieve.

B | Preposition collocations

Certain verbs are used more commonly in academic writing. These verbs are often more formal, and typically collocate with common prepositions such as *on*, *of* and *to*. These prepositions also commonly collocate with nouns and adjectives in other formal phrases.

1 Which sentence in each pair do you think is more likely to be in an academic text?

  a 1 This report will look at the organizational culture of Johnsons plc.

      2 This report will focus on the organizational culture of Johnsons plc.

  b 1 It's important to know about the impact that cultural differences can have within a multinational company.

      2 It's important to be aware of the impact that cultural differences can have within a multinational company.

  c 1 The reaction was based on prior experience.

      2 The reaction was because of prior experience.

2 Use the prepositions in the list to complete the collocations in bold in sentences a–f.

  of on to

  a Their perceived reality and **understanding** _____ the situation provokes differing reactions.

  b Good communication is **key** _____ effective teamwork.

  c Culture has a major **influence** _____ an individual's views.

  d The study emphasized the **impact** _____ individual differences on perception.

  e Culture is **at the root** _____ how people understand the world around them.

  f The **significance** _____ politeness within their culture cannot be ignored.

Writing skills

Taking notes and then expanding them to form complete sentences is a way of integrating others' work into your own. Using such a technique ensures that the ideas will be expressed in a similar style to your own writing, and helps you to avoid plagiarism.

A | Taking notes from a text

1 Look back at paragraph B in the text on page 5. Compare the notes below. Does the meaning change?

> INDIVIDUALS + PERCEPTION = diff. unique image of world
> analyse and judge info. received
> PERCEPTION = key in org. behaviour
> e.g. email to mgr on overtime in Dept > 4 interpretations –
> 1 reasonable request – improved staffing
> 2 unreasonable – mgement want more control
> 3 no objection – suspicious why
> 4 +ve – reduced costs + improved efficiency
> individ. experience = diff. perception

2 The notes in 1 use common techniques:

- using abbreviations
- using key content words
- simplifying complex sentences

Find two examples of each technique in the notes.

3 Write abbreviations for words a–e from the text.

perception   *perc.*

a language _____
b leader _____
c understanding _____
d process _____
e communication _____

4 Look back at paragraph A in the text.

a Circle at least ten key content words. What part of speech are these words (e.g. nouns, verbs)?
b Choose two complex sentences that you think it would be useful to simplify.

Compare in pairs.

5 Write notes for paragraphs C, D and E in the text. Focus on using abbreviations and key content words, and simplifying complex sentences.

6 In groups of three, each person give a spoken summary of one paragraph using their notes.

B | Expanding notes

1 Look at the notes and the sentence that follows. Then find the original sentence in the text on page 5 (para. A, lines 8–10).

> words + look + body lang. comm. view of world

Our words, appearance and body language communicate our view of the world.

Circle true (T) or false (F).

a The meaning is the same.   T / F
b The structure is the same.   T / F
c The idea is expressed in original language.   T / F

2 Look again at the notes on paragraph B in A1. Expand each part to make a complete section.

> INDIVIDUALS + PERCEPTION = diff. unique image of world

Individual perceptions mean that each person has a different and unique view of the world.

a	analyse and judge info. received
b	PERCEPTION = key in org. behaviour
c	e.g. email to mgr on overtime in Dept > 4 interpretations –
d	1 reasonable request – improved staffing
e	2 unreasonable – mgement want more control
f	3 no objection – suspicious why
g	4 +ve – reduced costs + improved efficiency
h	individ. experience = diff. perception

3 Look at your notes for another paragraph of the text.

- Expand your notes to form complete sentences.
- Compare your sentences to the original text. Have you kept the same meaning? Have you expressed the idea originally?

Research task

Organizations, leadership and behaviour vary in countries around the world. Research a culture different from your own. Make notes about that culture. What challenges might people from each culture face working together?

2 Motivation

Study focus

1 Rank the following rewards in order from 1 (most motivating) to 7 (least motivating) for you.

a cash bonus ____ a free meal ____

praise ____ certificates ____

promotion ____ medals ____

time off ____

2 Compare in pairs. What rewards would you use to motivate your employees?

Reading strategies

A | Understanding main ideas

1 Quickly read the extract from an academic textbook. Who created the expectancy theory of motivation?

2 Look at the structure of the text. Identify the main sections.

3 Match three paragraphs to phrases 1–3.

1 Valuing the reward. ____

2 Performance will lead to reward. ____

3 Effort will lead to performance. ____

4 Read paragraphs A and F, which describe expectancy theory. Choose the correct option to make statements a–c true.

a Expectancy theory is *an effort theory* / *a motivation theory*.

b Expectancy theory says that we consider three issues *before* / *after* we decide how to perform in certain situations.

c Expectancy theory says that we make a decision based on *one combined judgement* / *three separate judgements* of a given situation.

5 Match main ideas 1–4 to paragraphs B–E in the text.

Expectancy theory involves …

1 considering both the positive and the negative results of doing a task successfully. ____

2 assessing how much a reward is worth to us. ____

3 weighing up the types of rewards available and whether we are interested in them. ____

4 considering the amount of effort necessary to complete a task. ____

B | Understanding key phrases

1 Read the sentence highlighted in paragraph B (lines 10–12). Which of these could be defined as a 'resource'?

ability   time   money   effort

2 Read the sentence highlighted in paragraph C (lines 33–36). Define 'outcomes'. Give examples from the text of positive and negative outcomes.

3 Read paragraph D. Explain 'extrinsic rewards' (line 59) and 'intrinsic rewards' (line 66).

4 Read the sentence highlighted in paragraph E (lines 81–83). Which is the best synonym for 'valence'?

interest   bonus   value

C | Interpreting graphically presented data

1 Look at Figures 1 and 2 in the text. Which:

a shows an overview of the theory?

b relates to a specific section of the text?

2 Statements 1–3 are opinions expressed at different stages on the flow chart in Figure 1. Match 1–3 to letters A–C on the chart.

1 'To be honest, I'm not that motivated by praise.' ____

2 'Even though I have the ability to do the work, I don't think it will result in the promotion I want.' ____

3 'I very much doubt I have the ability to complete the task.' ____

3 Look at Figure 2 again. Tick the correct answer.

The table …

a is needed to understand part of the text. ____

b gives more examples of something that is in the text. ____

c explains something that is not in the text. ____

D | Reacting to the text

Which statements are true for you? Discuss in pairs.

- I feel demotivated if I don't have the skills or resources to complete something.
- I am more motivated by extrinsic rewards than intrinsic ones.
- Negative outcomes, such as losing leisure time, have a big negative impact on my motivation.

Expectancy theory

A The expectancy theory of motivation, originally proposed by Victor H. Vroom, argues that we consider three main points before we make the effort necessary to perform at a given level. These issues are shown
5 in the circles of Figure 1, which shows the basic components of expectancy theory.

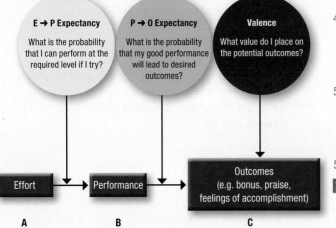

Figure 1 Basic components of expectancy theory

B **Effort-performance expectancy** When we consider **effort-performance expectancy** we assess the probability that our efforts will lead to the required
10 performance level. Our assessment may include evaluating our own abilities, as well as considering factors such as the availability of resources. To see how effort-performance expectancy works, imagine that your boss has asked you to consider taking on a major
15 special project. The project involves designing and implementing a new computerized tracking system for customer complaints, to improve individual customer service and find out more quickly about complaint trends. One of the first things you might think about is
20 the probability of your being able to achieve the high level of performance required, given your abilities and the related environmental factors. If you feel that you don't know very much about developing such systems and/or that the availability of resources is inadequate,
25 you might assess the probability of success as low. On the other hand, if you feel that you are well qualified for the project and that the available resources are adequate, you might assess the probability of your efforts' leading to high performance – the E→P
30 expectancy – as quite high. However, assessment of the effort-performance expectancy is only part of your evaluation of the situation.

C **Performance-outcome expectancy** With **performance-outcome (P→O) expectancy**, we assess
35 the probability that our successful performance will lead to certain outcomes. The major outcomes we consider are potential rewards (such as a bonus, a promotion, permission to leave early or a good feeling of accomplishment), although we are likely also to
40 take into account possible negative results (such as loss of leisure time or family disruption due to putting in extra hours on the job). In your special-project situation, perhaps your boss has a history of giving rewards, such as recognition or bonuses, to individuals
45 who take on special projects. If so you might assess the P→O expectancy for taking on the project as very high. On the other hand, your past experience with special projects may suggest that the boss sometimes arranges for rewards but other times forgets. If this
50 is the case, you might view the P→O expectancy as medium in strength (perhaps a 50-50 probability of being rewarded). In the worst case, if your boss never rewards extra effort, you might assess the P→O expectancy as almost zero – at least for rewards
55 available from the boss.

D In any given situation, there may be many potential rewards associated with performance. Rewards provided by others, such as bonuses, awards, or promotions, are known as **extrinsic rewards**. In
60 addition to monetary rewards, there are many types of non-monetary rewards that managers can provide to improve motivation (for some ideas, see the table in Figure 2). On the other hand, rewards that are related to our own internal experiences with
65 successful performance, such as feelings of achievement, challenge, and growth, are known as **intrinsic rewards**. Considering various possible outcomes (both positive

✔ Weekend trips to resorts	✔ Briefcases
✔ Time off	✔ "Boss of the day"
✔ Banquets	✔ President's Medallion
✔ Luncheons	✔ Free meals (on-the-spot award)
✔ Tickets to local events	✔ Cookouts
✔ Publicity (company and external)	✔ Attendance at outside seminars or conferences
✔ Certificates of recognition	✔ Photo session with company president
✔ "Travelling" awards (monthly)	
✔ Plaques	✔ Popular company logo items (T-shirts, gym bags, coffee mugs, pen-and-pencil sets, jackets, stadium chairs, ice chests, umbrellas, thermos jugs, paper weights, desk pen sets, leather goods)
✔ Special parking spaces	
✔ Free parking (in large cities)	
✔ Shopping sprees	
✔ Books, tapes, or videos	
✔ Family photo sessions	(K. H. "Skip" Wilson, Senior Training Specialist, Mississippi Power & Light Company)
✔ Trophies	
✔ Redeemable "Atta-boys/girls"	

Figure 2 A table showing non-monetary rewards

Source: Reprinted from Bob Nelson, *1001 Ways to Reward Employees*, Workman Publishing, New York, 1994, pp.44–45.

and negative), we form an assessment of the probability of our performance's leading to desired outcomes. If
70 our assessment of the P→O expectancy is high, the expectancy will contribute to our motivation. If our assessment is low, the expectancy could have a negative effect on our willingness to perform at a high level. Still, we have another motivational component to consider –
75 how important the various outcomes are to us.

E **Valence** With the **valence** component, we assess the anticipated value of various outcomes. If the available rewards interest us, valence will be high. However, the value of possible negative outcomes, such as the loss
80 of free time or the effect on our family, may offset the value of rewards in a given situation. The available rewards will only motivate when we attach a high overall valence to the situation. In the special-project example, you might view the possibility of a special
85 bonus from the boss in an extremely positive light. On the other hand, if your rich aunt just left you $3 million, the bonus may be much less important. Still you may

attach a high value to the intrinsic rewards that might result if you develop the innovative project.

F Expectancy theory argues that in deciding whether or not to make an effort in a particular direction, we will consider all three elements: E→P expectancy, P→O expectancy, and valence. Research suggests that individuals are likely to make global judgements about
95 each of the three elements in a given situation and then combine the elements in different ways.

Source: K Bartol & DC Martins, *Management*, Irwin/McGraw-Hill America 1998, pp.392–395

Glossary

component (line 6): (n) part
offset (line 80): (v) balance one thing against another so that there is less difference
leave (line 86): (v) give something when you die
element (line 92): (n) part

Business vocabulary

| Word formation: common endings

Identifying the part of speech can help you to understand a sentence and the meaning of a word in that sentence. Common endings such as -ive, -ion, -al and others can help identify the part of speech.

1 **What common word endings can you think of? Put them into the category that they usually appear in.**

Noun	-tion
Verb	-ate
Adjective	-al
Adverb	-ly

2 **Look at words a–h from the text on page 9. Underline the suffix in each word.**

expect<u>ancy</u> (line 1)   *(n)*

a performance (line 7)   _____
b quickly (line 18)   _____
c environmental (line 22)   _____
d permission (line 38)   _____
e accomplishment (line 39)   _____
f negative (line 40)   _____
g willingness (line 73)   _____
h motivate (line 82)   _____

3 **Are words a–h in 2 nouns (n), verbs (v), adjectives (adj) or adverbs (adv)?**

4 **Are the words in the list nouns, verbs, adjectives or adverbs?**

accomplish	assessment	environmentally
expectation	motivational	negatively
perform	permit	

5 **Change the words in the list to complete a–f.**

accomplishment	environmental	expectancy
motivation	performance	permission

a Many people _____ rewards to be at least equal to or greater than their effort.
b A variety of non-monetary rewards can be used to _____ people.
c The _____ in which people work can have an effect on their motivation.
d Despite _____ to the best of his ability the project was not considered a success.
e Smoking is not _____ in the building.
f She _____ the task as well as she could but unfortunately it was not satisfactory.

6 **Correct the word form errors in sentences a–f.**

a The staff were very unmotivation by their tasks.
b One of the greatest accomplish of her career was promotion to the top of her sector.
c A strong perform can lead to promotion.
d The decision impacted environmental on the town's development.
e The expect of a high salary is often a motivation for going to university.
f He was given permit to leave early.

Writing skills

A | Preparing for summary writing

Writing summaries can be an effective method of helping you start to select the main ideas of a text. It is also a step towards putting an idea in your own words for later use in writing.

1 Which statements a–g are true for a good summary? Circle T (true) or false (F).

a	It includes main ideas.	T / F
b	It includes your own ideas.	T / F
c	It includes minor details.	T / F
d	It is significantly shorter.	T / F
e	It includes repeated information.	T / F
f	It includes your own opinion.	T / F
g	It includes synonyms or changes of word form.	T / F

2 Write a summary label for word groups a–d.

Maths, Economics, Chemistry, Law = *Subjects*

a Finance, Human Resources, Accounts, Sales, IT
= _____

b train, plane, tram, tube, bus
= _____

c Prime Minister, President, CEO, Captain, Director
= _____

d lawyer, politician, teacher, accountant, doctor
= _____

3 Look at a sentence from the text on page 9 (line 15). Which are crossed out: 'content' words or 'non-content' words?

> ~~The~~ project involves ~~designing and implementing a new~~ computerized tracking ~~system for~~ customer complaints, ~~to improve individual customer~~ service.

4 Cross out some non-content words in sentences 1–3 from the text.

1 With performance-outcome expectancy we assess the probability that our successful performance will lead to certain outcomes. (lines 33–36)

2 Rewards that are related to our own internal experiences with successful performance, such as feelings of achievement, challenge, and growth, are known as intrinsic rewards. (lines 63–66)

3 However, the value of possible negative outcomes, such as the loss of free time or the effect on our family, may offset the value of rewards in a given situation. (lines 78–81)

5 In sentences 1–3 in 4, highlight content words which you could replace with similar words.

> ~~The~~ project involves ~~designing and implementing a new~~ computerized tracking ~~system for~~ customer complaints ~~to~~ improve ~~individual customer~~ service.

6 Write a summary of each sentence 1–3 in 4 using the fewest possible words.

> *The project involves computer tracking of complaints for better customer service.*

B | Using topic sentences

A topic sentence is often the first or second sentence in a paragraph. It carries the 'main idea', so a summarized topic sentence acts as a paragraph summary. You can link paragraph summary sentences to form a summary paragraph of the text. (Note that not all paragraphs have a clear topic sentence.)

1 Look back again at the text on page 9. Tick the paragraphs that have a clear topic sentence that includes the main idea of the whole paragraph.

Topic sentence

Paragraph A	☐	Paragraph D	☐
Paragraph B	☐	Paragraph E	☐
Paragraph C	☑	Paragraph F	☐

2 Choose one of the topic sentences you identified in 1. Summarize it using the technique in A3–5.

3 Decide how to summarize one of the paragraphs that has no clear topic sentence. Use content words to help you.

4 Compare your summary sentences in pairs. Then read each related paragraph of the text again, and adjust the wording of your sentences so that they are as good a summary as possible.

5 Now summarize the whole text. Link your summary sentences to form one summary paragraph. Read your summary paragraph to a partner.

Research task

Many theories have been written on motivation in the work place. Research another, different, theory of motivation. Write a summary of the main ideas.

3 The future of management

Study focus

1 When you hear the words 'honesty' and 'ethics', what jobs do you think of? Make a list.

2 Rank the following jobs in order from 'most honest' to 'least honest'. Discuss your reasons in pairs.

banker
builder
building contractor
business manager
lawyer
plumber
real estate agent
union leader

▲ most honest
_____
_____
_____
_____
_____
_____
_____
▼ least honest

Reading strategies

A | Identifying general point of view

1 Read the extract from a business magazine. Which statement, a, b or c, best completes the summary of the text?

Management …

a needs to be completely revised.

b in its traditional sense has no place in the future workplace.

c needs to be evaluated and changes made depending on the individual context.

2 Read the text again. Circle T (true) or F (false) for paragraphs A–H.

A People's opinions of managers are generally positive today. **T / F**

B The perception of management today does not match the traditional definition of management. **T / F**

C Traditional management theories are based on management in an industrial era. **T / F**

D Management and leadership are the same. **T / F**

E Management has changed dramatically in recent years and is continuing to do so. **T / F**

F Technology will not change the processes of management. **T / F**

G The author believes that a completely new method of management is needed. **T / F**

H The right choice depends very much on the individual situation. **T / F**

B | Identifying detailed point of view

Read paragraphs A–H again carefully. <u>Underline</u> one phrase or sentence in the text that matches the following points of view.

A Management can be improved by going back to the ideas at the foundation of management.

B Management involves getting groups to meet targets that individuals could not meet.

C Success today requires management that differs from the original roles of managers.

D People need both to lead others, and to manage day-to-day work; these are different and important roles.

E Management is about how people have always interacted.

F Management needs to change depending on the situation so it is likely to continue to evolve.

G A better understanding of management will allow for better decisions.

H Unfortunately, there isn't a simple formula for creating a more effective form of management.

C | Reacting to the text

1 Identify in the text at least three more roles or activities for a 'leader' and three more for a 'manager'. Note them below. Which do you think are most important?

to innovate   *to budget*

2 Complete your own definitions of the difference between a 'leader' and a 'manager'. Write examples. Compare in pairs.

- A manager is someone who …
  Example: _____

- A leader is someone who …
  Example: _____

3 Is the role of a 'manager' viewed positively or negatively in your country?

Management: back to basics

A In a 2008 Gallup survey on honesty and ethics among workers in 21 different professions, only 12% of respondents felt business executives had high/very high integrity – an all-time low. With a 37% low/very
5 low rating, the executives came in behind lawyers, union leaders, real estate agents, building contractors, and bankers. What should we do about this? Some observers would like us to change the word 'manager' altogether, favoring terms like leader, coach and
10 entrepreneur. But I believe a more useful approach is to reinvent management – to go back to basic principles of what management is all about. We need to help executives work out the best way to manage, and to help employees to get the managers they deserve.

Management versus leadership

B Let's start with a definition: Management is the act of getting people together to accomplish desired goals and objectives. Much is missing from this definition: no mention of planning, organization, staffing, controlling, or budgeting; no mention of companies or corporations;
20 and nothing about hierarchy or bureaucracy. And that is the point – management simply involves getting people to come together to achieve goals that they could not achieve on their own. But over the last century, the term management has changed into something narrower, and
25 more negative. Managers are often seen as low-level bureaucrats who are internally focused, engaged in operational details and controlling and coordinating the work of their subordinates.

C Why has this change in perception taken place? One
30 reason is that our way of thinking and talking about management is based on the century-old form of management practiced in large industrial firms. This approach to management was all about improving efficiency, standardization and quality control, and it
35 was built on principles of hierarchy, bureaucracy and extrinsic rewards. However, these objectives are not what drive success in most sectors today – we are much more likely to be concerned about innovation, speed and engagement. And yet we are still, for the
40 most part, using these industrial-era concepts to shape the way we get work done.

D To make room for leadership, experts felt they had to reduce the role of management. John Kotter saw managers as being the ones who plan, budget, organize,
45 and control, while leaders set direction, manage change, and motivate people. Leadership is a process of social influence: it is concerned with the traits, styles, and behaviors of individuals that cause others to follow them. Management is the act of getting people together
50 to accomplish desired goals. We all need to be leaders and managers: we need to be able to influence others through our ideas, words, and actions, and we also need to be able to get work done through others on a day-to-day basis.

What is the future of management?

E In the face of all these challenges, can management be reinvented to make it more effective as an agent of economic progress and more responsive to the needs of employees? Some say it can't. Henry Mintzberg argues in his most recent book, *Managing*, that the
60 nature of managerial work has not changed noticeably in the 40 years he has been studying it. Management is fundamentally about how individuals work together, and the basic laws of social interaction are not open to dramatic change. Indeed, it's interesting to note
65 that most of the major innovations in management – the industrialization of R&D, mass production, decentralization, brand management, discounted cash flow – occurred before 1930. If we extend this logic, we could conclude that the evolution of management
70 has more or less run its course; that, to use Francis Fukayama's famous expression, we've reached 'the end of history' with regard to management progress.

F But we haven't. Of course there is some validity in arguing that the basic laws of human behavior are not
75 going to change. But management practices are largely dependent on context, and as the nature of business organizations evolves, so too will management. Another school of thought says we are about to invent a new model of management, largely because of the information
80 technology revolution. However, we have been here before. All the arguments around decentralization and empowerment have been debated for a very long time.

G Is there a third way here? I believe there is. We don't need to create a whole new model of management –
85 there are many ideas from theory and practice to guide us. We need to develop a more detailed understanding of what management is about to make better choices. By going back to a basic definition of management – the act of getting people together to accomplish desired
90 goals – we can frame our discussion of the activities and principles of management much more clearly. My view is that you should take a more critical look at those choices. This involves four steps:
1. Understanding: You need to be explicit about the
95 management principles you are using to run your company. These principles are invisible, and often understood only at a subconscious level, but they drive the day-to-day processes and practices.
2. Evaluating: You need to assess whether your
100 company's management principles are suited to the business environment in which you are working. There are risks associated with whatever principles you employ, so you need to understand the pros and cons of each one so that you can choose wisely.

105 **3. Envisioning**: You need to seek out new ways of working, by looking at examples from different industries and from new contexts.

4. Experimenting: You need to be prepared to try out these practices in a low-risk way to see how they work.

H Alas, there is no recipe book for reinventing management. While these steps suggest a process for evaluating and rethinking your management principles, there is only so much you can learn from the mistakes made by troubled companies or from the latest Dilbert
115 cartoon. The right choices depend entirely on the specific circumstances and opportunities that your company faces, and on your willingness to experiment with unproven practices.

Source: *Fortune Magazine* by Julian Birkinshaw, 2010, London Business School

Glossary

Gallup (line 1): (proper n) an organization in the UK that conducts surveys
integrity (line 4): (n) honesty
engagement (line 39): (n) involvement
trait (line 47): (n) personal characteristic
run its course (line 70): (v phrase) will not develop or change anymore
school of thought (line 78): (n phrase) group of people with the same ideas or perspective

Business vocabulary

A | 'Management' and 'leadership'

1 Look at words/phrases a–k from the text. In pairs, decide what part of speech they are.

bureaucracy = noun

a standardization
b hierarchy
c to plan
d to budget
e to organize
f to control
g to manage change
h to motivate
i individual traits
j individual style
k to influence others

2 Explain the words/phrases in 1 to your partner. Give an example as part of your explanation.

bureaucracy – a system of controlling and operating an organization

3 Choose the correct option.

a It is essential to *budget / plan* a project to make sure it is finished at the right time.

b Her *individual style / trait* is to motivate people by giving a lot of praise.

c He likes to *control / motivate* everything, so his staff do not feel that they have any power.

d She was brought in to *organize / manage change* after the merger.

e The company has a very fixed clear *hierarchy / standardization*, with multiple levels.

f *Bureaucracy / Influencing others* is not productive, and is often seen as negative.

4 Are a–f in 3 related to leadership or management?

5 Write two or three sentences describing the role of a manager.

B | Change

The following expressions describe ideas of 'change'.

1 Complete the table with the expressions in the list to indicate the type of change.

to change noticeably
to move on
to reinvent
a small shift
a whole new model
to go back to basics
to progress
a minor development
a step forward

BIG change	little **change**
movement forwards →	movement backwards ←

2 Replace phrases a–d in *italics* with phrases in the correct form from 1.

a There have been only *a few changes* in management in the last 40 years.

b The company decided that *to return to a simple method of management* would be beneficial.

c Most new ideas do not *change* management *significantly* because people largely stay the same over time.

d Bureaucracy is seen by many not as a *development* but as a return to traditional methods.

3 Write four sentences describing changes in lifestyle. Use as many expressions from 1 as you can.

Writing skills

A | Analysing questions

Analysing an essay question is key to understanding exactly what a task is asking you to do. This involves breaking the question into different parts and understanding the main instruction word.

1 An essay question often contains several parts. Identify question parts a–d in these essay questions.

> Examine IBM's corporate strategy.

> Examine the changes in IBM's corporate strategy.

> Examine the changes in IBM's corporate strategy in Europe.

  a **Main topic**: the general area the question is about
  b **Focus**: a particular way to look at a topic
  c **Instruction**: one word or phrase that tells the writer what to do
  d **Limitation**: the specific area of the subject matter

2 How does adding each part change the focus of the essay question?

3 Look at essay questions a–f. Identify the different question parts.

  a Discuss Kotter's theories of leadership.
  b Compare and contrast the management style of IBM and Google in the 1990s.
  c Analyse the changes in leadership style during the last century.
  d 'Management' is bureaucratic, 'leadership' is inspirational. To what extent do you agree?
  e Define 'management', indicating its general scope and function.
  f Analyse the differences in leadership style between the USA and Japan.

B | Understanding instructions

1 What are the different expectations of the student in essay questions a and b? Compare your ideas in pairs.

  a   Describe Kotter's leadership theory.

  b   Evaluate Kotter's leadership theory.

2 Match essay question words a–f to definitions 1–6.

  a Define …   ____
  b Evaluate …   ____
  c Discuss …   ____
  d Justify …   ____
  e Outline …   ____
  f To what extent …? ____

  1 How much, for example, do you agree or disagree with (something)?
  2 Look at the strengths and weaknesses in (something).
  3 Write in detail about (something) looking at alternative viewpoints.
  4 Explain the exact meaning of (something).
  5 Give a good and acceptable reason for (something).
  6 Give brief main details of (something).

C | Developing research questions

After analysing and understanding an essay question, the next stage is to develop research questions. These will help you to focus your reading and research.

1 Look at the essay question and research questions a–e. Add two more possible questions.

> Evaluate Kotter's leadership theory.

  a What is Kotter's theory in general?
  b When was it written?
  c What is its specific focus?
  d What are the strengths and weaknesses of the theory?
  e What is the status of the theory today?
  f _____
  g _____

2 Make a list of research questions that you might need to ask about these essay questions before conducting your research.

> Examine the changes in IBM's corporate strategy in Europe.

> Analyse the changes in leadership style during the last century.

Research task

Look at some of the essay questions you have answered in your first language. Can you apply the essay question analysis principles from this lesson to those questions?

4 Marketing

Study focus

1 In pairs, discuss what you know about these international companies.

2 Answer the questions.

1 Do these companies have just one product or many different products?

2 How many different products can you think of for the four companies? Make a list for each.

3 Look at the phrase from the text and its definition.

> **portfolio of products** (line 1)

A range of products owned by one company or organization.

Think of a company you know well. Make notes about its portfolio of products.

Reading strategies

A | Understanding a text using background knowledge

1 You are going to read an extract from an academic textbook about Marketing. Of the products you wrote down in *Study focus*, which ones are the most successful now?

2 How do you think a company can evaluate the success of its products?

3 Which of the following characteristics is most important for a product to be successful? Rank them in order from 1 (most important) to 5 (least important).

to be new	____
to be established	____
to be old	____
to have a large share of the market	____
to be very profitable	____

4 What balance of the characteristics in 3 do you think a company needs in its portfolio of products?

5 Read the text and check your answers.

B | Understanding the relationship between text and graphic

1 Look at Figure 4.1 in the reading text.

a What does this figure show?

b How easy is this figure to interpret without reading the text?

2 Read the text again.

a In which paragraph can you find information about the origins of Figure 4.1?

b What additional information does the rest of the text provide about Figure 4.1?

3 Look at Figure 4.2 in the reading text.

a After studying Figure 4.1, is it easier to interpret Figure 4.2 without reading the text?

b What additional information does the text add about Figure 4.2?

C | Finding support for an opinion

1 Read opinions A–G. Then read each paragraph in more detail to find support for each opinion.

A The success of a product can only really be judged in relation to other products a company has.

B The success of a product doesn't depend only on market share.

C The rate of growth in some industries is likely to be higher than in others.

D Products that are already a market leader require a lot of investment to grow.

E A product that has low market share and low growth should be cut if it is unprofitable.

F Too many products in one category creates an unbalanced portfolio.

G The Boston Box cannot be used to solve a problem.

2 Think about one of the companies you focused on in *Study focus*. Where would their different products fit on the Boston portfolio matrix?

D | Reacting to the text

Discuss in pairs.

• What type of company could not use this model?

• Are all products and ideas developed rationally?

• What are the dangers for a company that has an unbalanced portfolio?

Product portfolio analysis

A When managing a collection or portfolio of products, it is important to realize that understanding the performance of an individual product can often fail to give the complete picture. What is really important is an understanding of the performance of a company's products relative to each other. By creating a balanced portfolio of old, mature, established, growing, and very new products, there is a better chance of delivering profits, both now and in the future.

B Assessing the variety of a company's products can be done in a number of ways. One method involves the creation of a two-dimensional graphic of their comparative strategic positions. This technique is referred to as a portfolio matrix. The Boston Consulting Group (BCG) developed the original idea, and their matrix, the **Boston Box**, is shown at Figure 4.1. It is based on two key variables, market growth and relative market share (i.e. market share as a percentage of the share of the product's largest competitor, expressed as a fraction). A relative share of 0.8 means that the product achieves 80 per cent of the market leader's sales volume (or value). This is not the strongest competitive position, but it is not a weak position either. A relative market share of 1 means that the company shares market leadership equally with a competitor. A relative market share of 2 means that it has twice the market share of its nearest competitor.

C In Figure 4.2, the vertical axis refers to the product's market growth rate and the horizontal axis refers to its market strength, as measured by relative market share. The size of the circles represents the sales revenue generated by the product. Relative market share is generally regarded as high when you are the market leader (i.e. when the relative market share is 1 or greater). Determining the rate of market growth of a product is more problematic and depends on the industry to some extent. In some industries a market growth rate of 5 per cent is regarded as high, whereas in others this might be 10 per cent. The benchmark between high and low is, however, often taken to be 10 per cent.

D The BCG identified four categories of product. *Question marks* (also known as 'problem children') are products that exist in growing markets but have low market share. As a result there is negative cash flow and they are unprofitable. *Stars* are probably market leaders, but their growth has to be financed through fairly heavy levels of investment. *Cash cows*, on the other hand, exist in fairly stable, low-growth markets and require little on-going investment. Their very high market share provides both positive cash flows and high levels of profitability. *Dogs* experience low growth, low market share, and generate negative cash flow. These performance indicators suggest that they are operating in declining markets and they have no real long-term future.

E Portfolio analysis is an important analytical tool as it draws attention to the cash flow and investment characteristics of a company's products and indicates how financial resources can be manoeuvred to attain optimal strategic performance over the long term. Essentially, excess cash generated by cash cows should be utilized to develop question marks and stars, which are unable to support themselves. This enables stars to become cash cows and therefore be self-supporting assets.

F Dogs should only be retained as long as they contribute to positive cash flow and do not restrict the use of assets and resources elsewhere in the business. Once they do, they should be divested or removed from the portfolio.

F Plotting all of a company's products on to the matrix, it becomes easier to see how well balanced the product portfolio is. An unbalanced portfolio is one that has too many products grouped in one or two quadrants. Where products are distributed equally, and where market shares and cash flows equate with their market position, the portfolio is said to be financially healthy and well balanced.

G Portfolio analysis is an important guide to strategic development, because it gives answers to questions like:
How will the market grow?
What will be our market share?
What investment will be required?
How can a balanced portfolio be created from this point?
However, the Boston Box only provides strategic indicators, not solutions. It is management's task to consider the information and make decisions based on their judgement.

Source: P Baines, C Fill & K Page, *Marketing*, Oxford University Press 2008, pp.79–83

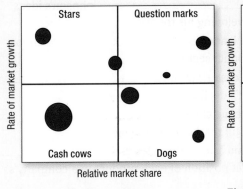

Figure 4.1 The Boston Box

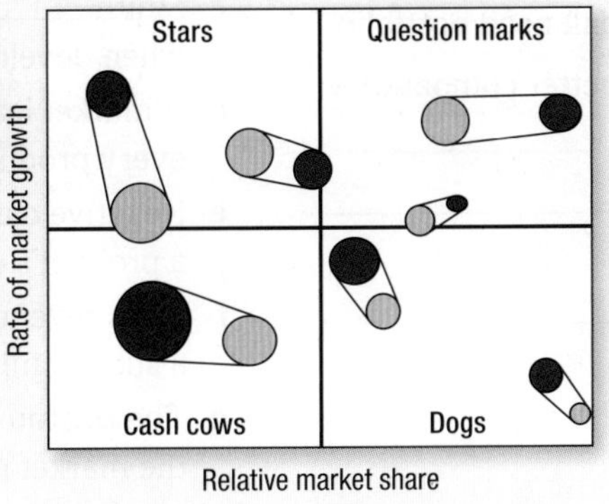

Figure 4.2 Present and future positions in the BCG matrix

Business vocabulary

A | Marketing

1 Check you understand key marketing terms from the text on page 17. Replace the phrases in *italics* in sentences 1–7 with phrases a–g.

  a a balanced portfolio (line 5)
  b comparative strategic position (line 10)
  c relative market share (line 17)
  d the market leader (line 25)
  e sales revenue (line 23)
  f rate of market growth (line 26)
  g negative cash flow (line 38)

  1 Our *proportion of the market* compared to our rivals is weakening.
  2 Our *increase in the share of business* has been larger than many competitors.
  3 The importance of *a product in comparison to our other products* is key to each product succeeding.
  4 If a company has too many similar products, the products will compete against each other. Every company needs *a good range of products* to sell to consumers.
  5 Our soft drink is *number one* in the drinks market.
  6 Our *income from selling* has been strong this year.
  7 We have *more money going out than we have coming in*. If this continues we will go into debt.

2 Make sentences a–g true by completing them with the name of a company you know about. Explain your reasons.

  a In recent years the rate of market growth for _____ has been faster than its competitors.
  b _____ is the market leader.
  c _____ has problems with negative cash flow.
  d _____ has a balanced portfolio.
  e _____ has a better comparative strategic position than _____ .
  f The relative market share of _____ is high.
  g The sales revenue of _____ is very high.

B | Verb–preposition collocations

Understanding and learning verb–preposition collocations will help you to use key expressions more accurately.

1 Match the prepositions in the list to the verbs they are commonly used with.

  to on by in

  a to base (something) _____
  b to refer _____
  c to depend _____
  d to exist _____
  e to draw attention _____
  f to be generated _____
  g to contribute _____
  h to plot (something) _____

2 Quickly look back at the text on page 17 and check your answers to 1.

3 Match verb–preposition collocations a–h in 1 to definitions 1–8.

  1 to mention another idea ____
  2 to use something to form an idea ____
  3 to mark something on a graph or chart ____
  4 to be reliant on, or need the support of, someone or something ____
  5 to be present in a place or market ____
  6 to come from, or be produced by, something ____
  7 to highlight the importance of something ____
  8 to add something else to something ____

4 Choose a collocation to complete sentences a–h.

  a The research was _____ a study of 500 people.
  b The success of a product often _____ the investment in it.
  c Smith _____ Johnson's ideas when developing his theory.
  d A market leader _____ almost every product sector.
  e Negative cash flow can _____ a product's decline.
  f Sales revenue can be _____ a successful marketing campaign.
  g The Boston Matrix theory is used to _____ the market position of each product in a company's portfolio.
  h Statistical data is often _____ a graph for the purposes of analysis.

Writing skills

To 'paraphrase' means to express what someone else has said or written using your own words. Being able to paraphrase a text shows that you have understood it. You can change:

1 word order/sentence structure
2 grammatical form, e.g. *understanding* (v) = *an understanding of* (n)
3 non-specialized vocabulary, e.g. *the complete picture = everything you need to know*

When you paraphrase someone else's work, the words and the structure change but the meaning stays the same.

A | Paraphrasing sentences

1 Look at sentences A and B. How are they similar? How are they different? Which sentence is from the text on page 17?

Sentence A

When managing a collection or portfolio of products, it is important to realize that understanding the performance of an individual product can often fail to give the complete picture. (29 words)

Sentence B

An understanding of the performance of a single product won't necessarily tell you everything you need to know, and if you are responsible for the management of a portfolio of products it is essential to recognize this fact. (38 words)

2 Look at sentence B in 1 again. Underline phrases in B that have the same meaning as words/phrases 1–5 from A circled below.

¹(When managing) a collection or portfolio of products, ²(it is important to realize) that ³(understanding) the performance of ⁴(an individual product) ⁵(can often fail to give the complete picture).

3 Tick what has changed from sentence A.

word order ___	punctuation ___
vocabulary ___	grammar ___
spelling ___	meaning ___

4 Which words/phrases in sentence A have not changed in sentence B? Why is this?

5 Which sentence, 1 or 2, best paraphrases sentence C from the text? Why is it the best?

Sentence C

Plotting all of a company's products on to the matrix, it becomes easier to see how well balanced the product portfolio is. (lines 62–66)

1 By plotting a company's products on the matrix, you can more easily see how balanced the portfolio is.
2 You can analyse whether or not a company's product portfolio is well balanced by comparing the individual products using the portfolio matrix.

6 Paraphrase sentences a–c. Change the word order and use a synonym for the underlined words.

It is considered to be a weakness if a company focuses too much on just one product.

If a company focuses too much on just one product it is seen to be a weakness.

a It is important for a company to recognize when one of its products is operating in a declining market.
b As far as possible, a company should know about the activities of its competitors.
c If a company is experiencing financial difficulties it is a good idea to conduct a portfolio analysis.

B | Writing practice

1 Look at the ideas highlighted in sentence D. Paraphrase it using the techniques in A1–6.

Sentence D

(Portfolio analysis is an important analytical tool) as it (draws attention to the cash flow and investment) (characteristics of a company's products) and indicates how (financial resources can be manoeuvred to attain) (optimal strategic performance) over the long term. (lines 40–48)

2 Paraphrase sentence E.

Sentence E

An unbalanced portfolio is one that has too many products grouped in one or two quadrants. Where products are distributed equally, and where market shares and cash flows equate with their market position, the portfolio is said to be financially healthy and well balanced. (lines 66–74)

Research task

Research a company with a suitable product range. Plot their key products on the Boston Box.

5 Management systems

Study focus

1 Think of a manager you have had. Was this manager a good manager? Why/Why not? Tell a partner.

2 Brainstorm what makes a good manager.

A good manager ...

Reading strategies

A | Reading for general understanding

In pairs, read the extract from an academic textbook on management theory. Find what these numbers refer to.

Student A Tell **B** about …

1 1841.
2 1860.
3 1888.
4 1949.

Student B Tell **A** about …

5 14.
6 19.
7 1918.
8 1925.

B | Understanding main and supporting ideas

1 Read paragraph A again. Which statement, a, b or c, best summarizes the main idea?

a The life of Henri Fayol.
b The origins of administrative management theory.
c A comparison of Fayol and Taylor's theories.

2 Find examples of the supporting ideas in paragraph A. Does the author …

a give extra details?
b give examples?
c give more explanation?

3 Read the rest of the text again.

a What is the main idea in paragraph **B**?
b What is the main idea in section **C**?

4 What techniques from 2 does the author use to support the main ideas in B and C?

C | Critical reading

Reading academic texts often requires a critical approach in order to understand and question the content. When you are reading a text critically, you need to, firstly, understand the key ideas, secondly, identify where the writer highlights weaknesses in those ideas, and finally, form your own opinion on the ideas.

1 Read section C in the reading text again. Which of Fayol's ideas do you think relate to the following groups? Write the 'Key ideas' numbers in the chart (some can be in more than one group).

	Principles
Roles	
Control / power	
Rewards for staff	
Equality	
Other?	

2 Are there any other groupings? Note them in the chart. How are the ideas similar? Compare in pairs.

3 Look at Fayol's first principle, 'Division of work'. How does he highlight a weakness in this key idea?

4 In pairs, look at four or five more of Fayol's principles.

a Does Fayol make any further comments?
b For each idea you looked at, can you think of a criticism or weakness?

5 Overall, what do you think of Fayol's theory of 'administrative management'?

D | Reacting to the text

If you were to select three of Fayol's principles to use in your working life, which ones would they be and why? Discuss in pairs.

Glossary

foundry (line 7): (n) factory in which metal is shaped into different objects
stimulate (line 14): (v) start up, create
absolute (line 23): (adj) with no exceptions
adapt (line 26): (v) change
obedience (line 40): (n) doing what you are told

Henri Fayol

A Managers are able to use the ideas of **administrative management** developed by Henri Fayol (1841–1925), whose work is similar to that of Taylor and Weber. Fayol trained as an engineer, graduating at the age of
5 19 as the best student in his year. In 1860 he joined Commentry-Fourchambault-Decazeville, a coal mining and iron foundry company, rising rapidly through the company to become managing director in 1888 (Parker and Ritson, 2005). By the time he retired in
10 1918 it had become one of the success stories of French industry. Throughout his career he kept detailed diaries and notes about his management experiences, and his thoughts on these formed the basis of his work after retirement. From these he sought to stimulate
15 discussion and thinking about management in both private and public sectors. His book, *Administration, industrielle et generale* only became widely available in English in 1949 (Fayol, 1949).

B Fayol credited his success as a manager to the methods
20 he used, not to his personal qualities. He believed that managers should use certain principles in performing their functions listed in the Key Ideas box. The term 'principles' did not suggest they were fixed or absolute:

> 'It is all a question of proportion…. allowance must
25 be made for different changing circumstances … the principles are flexible and can adapt to every need; it is a matter of knowing how to make use of them, which is a difficult art requiring intelligence, experience, decision and judgement.' (Fayol, 1949)

30 In using such terms as 'changing circumstances' and 'adapt to every need' in setting out the principles, Fayol anticipated the contingency theories that were developed in the 1960s.

Fayol's principles of management

Key Ideas

1 Division of work If people specialise, the more
35 they can concentrate on the same matters and so gain an ability and accuracy, which increases their output. However, 'it has limits which experience teaches us may not be exceeded'.

2 Authority and responsibility The right to give
40 orders and to demand obedience, based either on a manager's official authority or his or her personal authority. 'Whenever authority is exercised, responsibility arises.'

3 Discipline 'Essential for the successful operation
45 of business … without discipline no company can succeed.'

4 Unity of command 'For any action whatsoever, an employee should receive orders from one superior only' – to avoid conflicting instructions and
50 resulting confusion.

5 Unity of direction 'One head and one plan for a group of activities with the same objective … essential for joint action, co-ordination of strength and focusing of effort.'

55 **6 The importance of general interests over individual interests** 'The interests of one employee or group of employees should not be more important that the needs of the company.'

7 Payment given to staff 'Should be fair and, as far
60 as possible, give satisfaction both to personnel and firm.'

8 Centralisation 'The question of centralisation or decentralisation is a simple question. The share of initiative to be left to subordinates depends on
65 the character of the manager, the reliability of the subordinates and the condition of the business. The degree of centralization must vary according to different cases.'

9 Scalar chain 'The chain of superiors from the
70 main authority to the lowest … is often too lengthy in large organisations, especially governmental ones.' Fayol pointed out that if a quick decision was needed it was appropriate for people at the same level of the chain to communicate directly, as long
75 as their immediate superiors approved.

10 Order Materials should be in the right place in order to avoid loss, and the positions needed for the successful running of the business filled by capable people.

80 **11 Equity** Managers should be both friendly and fair to their subordinates – 'equity requires much good sense, experience and good nature.'

12 Secure jobs A high employee turnover is not efficient – 'The threat of unemployment is both the
85 cause and effect of the bad running of a company.'

13 Initiative 'Allowing all people to show initiative is a great source of strength for businesses … it is essential to encourage and develop this. The manager must be able to sacrifice some
90 personal vanity in order to give this satisfaction to subordinates … a manager able to do so is much superior to one who cannot.'

14 Esprit de corps 'Harmony, union among the personal of an organisation is a great strength
95 in that organisation. Effort should be made to establish it.'

Source: D Boddy, *Management, an introduction*, Pearson, Harlow 2007, pp.52–53

Business vocabulary

| Noun combinations to define or describe

Vocabulary patterns can help you to identify the type of text you are reading, which in turn helps you to understand the purpose of the writer. 'noun + *of* + noun' combinations is an example of a pattern that is common in texts which define and describe.

1 Match text types a–c to descriptions 1–3.

  a Comparative   ____

  b Descriptive   ____

  c Evaluative   ____

  1 In this kind of text, a judgement is made about how good, useful, or successful something is.

  2 In this kind of text, similarities and differences between two theories or ideas are examined. Some assessment of the relative importance of each may be necessary.

  3 In this kind of text, detailed information is given about someone or something.

2 **What type of text in 1 is the 'Henri Fayol' text on page 21?**

3 **Read the definitions of 'noun + *of* + noun' phrases 1–8 from the text. Complete them with a noun from the list.**

| business | initiative | management | the manager |
| strength | superiors | unemployment | work |

  1 idea of _____   a theory of supervision, organization, or administration

  2 division of _____   the sharing of tasks or responsibilities

  3 operation of _____   the process of running an organization

  4 share of _____   the division of enterprise or inventiveness

  5 character of _____   the personality of the person in control

  6 chain of _____   the links between managers or people in a position of authority

  7 threat of _____   the fear of losing a job

  8 source of _____   the origin of power or support

4 **Use noun patterns from 3 to complete sentences a–h.**

  a Google is an example of a democratic company where employees take a _____ . People are actively encouraged to work on new ideas.

  b An unfair _____ between people of equal levels in a company can be a cause of complaint among employees.

  c The _____ usually rises when an economy is in recession.

  d The size of the population in China is often seen as a negative factor; however, it has been a _____ in helping the economy grow quickly.

  e The successful _____ can depend on a number of factors such as the economy, competition, and dedication of the employees.

  f Large companies often have a long _____ because of the high number of levels in their hierarchy.

  g Many theories and _____ are based on personal and practical experience.

  h The _____ can have a major impact on the satisfaction of employees and the way in which a company is run.

5 **Choose three noun phrases from 3. Write your own example sentences.**

  a _____

     _____

  b _____

     _____

  c _____

     _____

Writing skills

Most paragraphs written in English follow a standard structure that includes a topic sentence, supporting ideas and concluding ideas. A paragraph often also includes a sentence to aid transition between paragraphs.

A | Paragraph structure

1 Read the paragraph below. Match parts 1–4 to section descriptions a–d.

> (1) The amount of payment given to staff needs to be carefully considered by management. (2) The chosen amount needs to be an adequate reflection of the skills of the staff member and the effort he/she puts into the job. If the payment is too low, staff will be demotivated, and will feel unappreciated by management. (3) However, the payment should not be dramatically higher than similar jobs at competitor companies, otherwise profit levels will be affected. (4) Essentially it is the task of management to make a measured and informed decision about levels of pay.

   a a short explanation to support the main idea   ___

   b a concluding sentence   ___

   c the identification of a weakness or problem   ___

   d a topic sentence giving the main idea of the paragraph   ___

2 Put sentences a–d into a logical paragraph order.

   a This is due to the fact that any team that works well together, one where team members have good relationships with each other, is more likely to be successful in achieving its targets.

   b In some cases, despite the best efforts of management, team members fail to work well together, and this has an impact on output.

   c It is common practice for management to try to generate an esprit de corps, or harmony, within their team.

   d Generating this harmony can be difficult if it does not exist naturally, and managers often look to team-building training programmes to bring about the desired change.

B | Transitioning between paragraphs

1 Look at an alternative final sentence for the paragraph in A1. What is different? How does this change the function of the final sentence?

> Essentially it is the task of management to make a measured and informed decision about levels of pay, and this can be achieved in a number of ways.

2 What would you expect the content of the next paragraph to cover?

3 Look again at the final sentence of the paragraph in A2. Change it to transition smoothly into a new paragraph.

C | Writing practice

1 Read the paragraph about 'Division of work' based on Fayol's first principle. Choose two of Fayol's other key ideas and expand them into complete paragraphs.

> **Division of work** If people specialise, the more they can concentrate on the same matters and so gain an ability and accuracy, which increases their output.
>
> > For example, a person who deals solely with customer complaints will become very specialised in dealing with these. They will be more efficient at handling them than other colleagues who do not deal with complaints. As a result this person will become more efficient and accurate and be of greater benefit to the company.
>
> However, 'it has limits which experience teaches us may not be exceeded'. (lines 34–38)

2 Exchange your paragraphs with a partner. Check that your partner has some or all of the following:

• a topic sentence
• a short explanation supporting the main idea
• a weakness or problem
• a concluding statement
• a transition sentence

Research task

Research another theory of the principles of management. What are the strengths and weaknesses of this theory?

6 Ethics

Study focus

Which is more important in a company, money or ethics? Put a cross on the line to show your opinion. Compare in pairs.

A company should aim to …

←———————————————————→

make money
in whatever
way it can.

be ethical
and socially
responsible.

Reading strategies

Headings often work with topic sentences to signpost the main ideas of a section or paragraph. Sometimes the main idea is expressed partly by the heading and partly by the topic sentence.

A | Understanding a text using headings

1 **Read section headings 1–3 in the extract from an academic textbook. Then quickly read the text.**

Which section …
a describes the view that businesses should work for the public good?
b describes the view that businesses should concentrate on creating wealth?
c describes different ideas about how businesses might behave responsibly?

2 **Read the headings of paragraphs B–E. Match topic sentences 1–4 to the correct paragraphs in the text.**

1 Society expects managers to obey the law – by not polluting rivers, selling faulty products or providing misleading information to investors. ___

2 Here managers focus on serving the economic interests of the company and its shareholders. ___

3 This covers actions that are entirely voluntary, not being shaped by economic, legal or ethical considerations. ___

4 This area includes actions that are not specified by law, and may not serve a company's narrow economic interests. ___

3 **Read paragraph F. Circle T (true) or F (false).**

a It has no connection to the paragraphs before. T / F
b It refers to a diagram that summarizes paragraphs A–E. T / F
c It discusses paragraphs A–E in detail. T / F
d It links the topics that came before with the topics that will come after. T / F
e It introduces a new focus that will be developed in the next paragraphs. T / F

B | Predicting content using topic sentences

1 **Read the bold topic sentences in paragraphs G–K. Identify one thing each paragraph will say.**

2 **Compare in pairs. Read again and check.**

3 **Circle T (true) or F (false) for statements a–b about each paragraph.**

G Friedman believed that …
a businesses should operate honestly to create wealth. T / F
b managers had both economic and ethical responsibilities. T / F

H Henderson believed that if companies take on the government's role of supporting social causes, it can …
a increase company profits in the long term. T / F
b cause economic damage. T / F

I Others think that companies should be socially responsible because …
a companies depend on society since they need customers, staff and social institutions. T / F
b if they aren't then all customers will stop buying from them. T / F

J Businesses are generally more socially responsible now because …
a the law tells them to be. T / F
b people in society expect and demand that they are. T / F

K What a company decides to do about social responsibility depends on …
a the sector they operate in and what competitors do. T / F
b their relationship with stakeholders in the business and in society. T / F

The role of business in society

1 Positioning corporate responsibility

A Figure 6.1 presents a way of analysing how managers can respond to ideas and opportunities of socially responsible behaviour. Four possibilities (Carroll, 1999) are in the scale, from economic responsibilities on the
5 left-hand side through to discretionary responsibilities on the other.

```
        ┌─────────────────────┐
        │  Criteria of corporate │
        │  social performance    │
        └─────────────────────┘
```

| Economic responsibility (make a profit) | Legal responsibility (obey the law) | Ethical responsibility (do what is right, avoid harm) | Discretionary responsibility (contribute to community, be philanthropic) |

Source: Carroll (1999)

Figure 6.1 Criteria of corporate social performance

B **Economic responsibilities**
　... They act to support that aim, regardless of the effects on communities or other considerations. An example was when Burberry, the clothes retailer,
10 decided to close one of its few remaining UK factories. The finance director was questioned by the media about the decision, and she said: 'Ultimately if a factory isn't commercially viable you have to take the decision to close ... that's what your obligations to your
15 shareholders dictate. When you know you've made the right decision commercially, you have to stay true to that. These are the facts – commercial realities reign'. (*Financial Times*, 15 February 2007, p3)

C **Legal responsiblities**
　... These issues reflect areas that society has decided
20 were important enough to make laws regulating company behaviour in the wider interest. Some companies will take these responsibilities seriously – but will go no further. If what they do is legal, then that is their only criterion – even if the decision has
25 damaging consequences for others.

D **Ethical responsibilities**
　... Managers take these actions because they believe they meet some wider social interest, such as discouraging tobacco consumption, protecting the natural environment or supporting a socially
30 disadvantaged group. They may do so in the belief that these will fit with their economic responsibilities by, for example, strengthening their reputation with customers or local communities. Announcements by companies such as Marks and Spencer or Tesco that they will trade
35 in a carbon-neutral way are examples.

E **Discretionary responsibilities**
　... They include money given with no expectation or possibility of getting the money back, sponsorship of local events and contributions to charities – the actions are entirely philanthropic. The decision by Innocent
40 to give 10 per cent of profits to charities such as the Rainforest Alliance is an example.

F While Figure 6.1 sets out the range of possible management policies, it offers no judgment on which of these they do, or should, follow. That choice
45 depends on how they respond to two views on the role of business in society. One is identified with Milton Friedman, a US economist who argued that the role of business is to create wealth. The other is based on the idea of corporate responsibility, where the emphasis is
50 on public good rather than private gain.

2 The Friedmanite position

G Milton Friedman was clear: 'In a free economy there is one and only one social responsibility of business – to use its resources to take part in activities designed to increase its profits so long as
55 it stays within the rules of the game, which is to say, takes part in open and free competition, without deception or fraud.' (1962, p.133) As an economist, Friedman believed that operating business 'without deception or fraud' provided sufficient social benefit
60 through the creation of wealth or employment. In terms of Figure 6.1, managers should concern themselves only with economic and legal responsibilities. For a business to give money away to charitable purposes was equivalent to self-imposed taxation. He argued that
65 the board of directors in charge of a business should concentrate on generating wealth for shareholders, and passing it on to them. Shareholders could then decide if they wished to use that income to support social causes (Margolis and Walsh, 2003).

H Henderson (2001) develops this view, arguing that for business to take on responsibilities which are in the field of government harms, rather than improves, human welfare. Others point out that meeting tough environmental or other regulations
75 increases costs, and makes a business less competitive than those operating in countries with less interest in the topic (Stavins, 1994). Investing in socially responsible but unprofitable projects will eventually damage a firm and so be unsustainable.

3 Corporate responsibility as a moral obligation

I Others disagree, taking the view that corporations have both the resources and the moral obligations to act in ways that benefit others – such as by making sure suppliers treat staff fairly, minimising environmental damage, treating customers honestly

85 **and giving generously to charity.** They maintain that while society depends on business for products and services, business in turn depends on society. It requires inputs – employees, capital and physical resources – and the socially created institutions that enable business to
90 operate – such as a legal and education system.

J **The moral case for corporate responsibility reflects this interdependency: society and business have mutual obligations within a social contract.** What people expect of companies changes. Pressure groups
95 can persuade governments to create laws to protect consumers from unwelcome selling practices or faulty products and services. Public demand for recycled or more environmentally friendly products has prompted changes in corporate behaviour and products.

K Taking a Friedmanite position implies a relatively simple rule for managers – do what is best for the business and the shareholders. The alternative view regards responsible corporate behaviour as a form of enlightened self-interest, in the sense that it can satisfy

105 both economic *and* moral expectations. Managers may add more value (and serve their shareholders better) if they interpret their responsibilities more widely than implied by the Friedmanite position, but do so in ways that bring economic benefits to business. Which
110 of these approaches managers adopt will reflect how they interpret the relative power and interests of their stakeholders.

....

Source: D Boddy, *Management, an introduction*, Pearson, Harlow 2007, pp.155–157

Glossary

viable (line 13): (adj) able to survive
reign (line 17): (v) have power
philanthropic (line 39): (adj) doing good things for other people
fraud (line 57): (n) cheating, unlawful activity
adopt (line 110): (v) begin to use

Business vocabulary

Noun collocations

Understanding and learning noun–noun collocations can help you to extend your core vocabulary.

1 **Match collocations 1–7 to definitions a–g. (1–5 are from the text on pages 24–26.)**

1 finance director (line 11) ___
2 economic interests (p.24, 2) ___
3 management policies (line 43) ___
4 human welfare (line 73) ___
5 education system (line 90) ___
6 HR department ___
7 sales target ___

a an organization's financial aims or concerns
b the health and happiness of people
c a person in charge of monetary matters in an organization
d the amount that a company wants to sell
e the organization of teaching and learning
f the section of a company that organizes everything connected to the staff
g the rules or strategies of the people in charge of a company

2 **Complete sentences a–g with a collocation from 1.**

a A company's _____ will affect its policies in areas such as ethical responsibility.

b The _____ plays a key role in any large organization as he/she has a major say in how money is spent.

c The _____ control how a company is run.

d Every year senior management decide on the _____ for the next year, and staff need to try and hit it.

e The _____ of many countries affects the age at which people can enter the labour market.

f The _____ deals with recruitment and training.

g It is unlikely that a company following a Friedmanite position will be concerned with _____ .

3 **Choose one word from each collocation in 1.**

a Add another word to create a new collocation.
   *marketing **director** / **finance** report*

b Use your new collocation in a new sentence.
   The marketing director is responsible for making a company's advertising fit the strategic aims of the organization.

Writing skills

Academic writing often includes contrast and comparison. Expressions such as *However, ...* and *In the same way, ...* are often used to start a second sentence to either contrast with or support the first sentence.

A | Describing similarity and difference

1 Look at the following paragraph. <u>Underline</u> three starting words that support or contrast with something that has gone before.

> A Friedmanite position believes that the sole purpose of a company is to make money. Conversely, some people believe that a company has a moral obligation to do more for society. A Friedmanite position argues that giving money to charity is the same as a self-imposed taxation. Similarly, Henderson believes that if companies invest their money in social issues it does not necessarily mean people's lives will improve, as there could be a negative impact on the company's finances. However, others argue that companies are dependent on society and should be obliged to give something back.

2 Put the <u>underlined</u> expressions from 1 in the table.

Expressing similarity	Expressing difference
In the same way, ...	

3 Choose one phrase from the table in 2 to start the second sentence in a–d.

a The culture in the south is quite conservative. _____ , the culture in the north is much more open.

b Online news pages are having an impact on newspaper sales. _____ , hand-held eBooks are affecting the sales of printed books.

c Companies and countries are trying to develop reusable energy. _____ , it is not widely available.

d During an economic downturn, accountants often find that their services are in demand. _____ , debt advisors find that they have more work during times of economic hardship.

4 Look again at the paragraph in 1. Which expression means '... *is like (something)*'?

5 Add the expressions in the list to the table in 2.

x is like   different from   the same as
both x and y are ...   x is ..., whereas y is ...   in contrast
on the one hand ... on the other hand

6 In pairs, add more phrases to the table in 2 to describe similarity or difference.

7 Choose the correct option.

a The role of a company is seen to be *the same as / compared with* the role of a government by some, and these people argue that just *whereas / like* governments, companies also have a moral obligation to society.

b A Friedmanite position sees the role of a company as *compared with / different from* that of government.

c As companies are dependent on society, some believe that *both / like* companies and governments have moral obligations.

d A Friedmanite position can be *compared with / different from* a capitalist approach to business *whereas / the same as* the alternative view is closer to communism in its approach.

B | Writing practice

1 Write two sentences comparing the things in a–c.
   a Mercedes / Hyundai
   b French food / Italian food
   c English weather / Japanese weather

2 Compare your sentences in pairs.

3 Write a paragraph comparing two business theories or approaches. Use your knowledge from your course or this book to help you.

4 Read your partner's paragraph. Compare it with yours. What are the similarities and differences?

Research task

Choose two companies you know well. Write a short comparison of the role they have in society.

Study focus

1 In pairs, in one minute, make a list of as many decisions as you can that you have to make in a day.

2 Why are decision-making strategies so crucial for managers today?

Reading strategies

A | Reading quickly for general understanding

1 Quickly read the extract from an academic textbook. Which statement, a, b or c, best completes a summary of the text?

The text describes …
  a the most effective way to make decisions in management.
  b and compares rational and non-rational decision-making.
  c and analyses the strengths and weaknesses of four different decision-making strategies.

2 Under which heading does the author group the Satisficing, Incremental and Garbage Can models?

rational   non-rational   decision-making

3 Match the models to strategies 1–4.

  the Rational model   the Incremental model
  the Satisficing model   the Garbage Can model

  1 In this model, managers will only look for an alternative until an acceptable solution is found.
  2 In this model, decisions happen by chance.
  3 This model solves only short-term problems.
  4 In this model, managers have all the right information to make the best decision.

B | Identifying the writer's point of view

1 Circle T (true) or F (false).

According to the writer …
  a the Rational model is still considered a very effective strategy to use.   T / F
  b the Satisficing model is considered useful mainly when decisions are simple and need to be quick. T / F
  c the Incremental model is considered effective for making long-term decisions.   T / F
  d the Garbage Can model suggests that decisions are made through analysis and calculation.   T / F

2 Underline in the text one strength and one weakness that the writer mentions for each model. Complete the table.

	Strength	Weakness
Rational model		
Satisficing model		
Incremental model		
Garbage Can model		

3 Does the writer mention the strength or the weakness first in each case? What does this tell us about his attitude to each model?

4 Rank the models in order from 1 (most effective) to 4 (least effective) according to how you think the writer would rate each in the decision-making process.

C | Reading closely for detailed information

Read the text again and answer the questions.
  1 According to the Rational model, on what basis do managers make decisions?
  2 Why is buying a car or a personal computer a good example of the difficulty of making optimal decisions?
  3 What did Herbert Simon base the Satisficing model on?
  4 What is the limitation of the Satisficing model?
  5 According to the Incremental model, why don't managers require a lot of information to make their decisions?
  6 What example of weakness in the Incremental model does the writer give?
  7 What four factors are decisions dependent on in the Garbage Can model?
  8 What mistake did William Ylvisaker make in his decision-making?

D | Reacting to the text

Think of a difficult decision you have had to make recently.

• How did you make that decision? Was your decision-making similar to one of the models in the text?
• Do you think your decisions generally follow one of the models in the text?

Rational and non-rational decision-making models

A The rational model of managerial decision making, a view that was popular during the first half of this century, has roots in the economic theory of the firm. In developing theories about the economic behaviour of business firms, economists tended to make the simple assumption that managers would always make decisions that were in the best economic interests of their firms. This assumption was initially accepted by many management theorists. According to the **rational model**, managers use completely rational decision processes, in the end make optimal decisions, and possess and understand all information that is important to their decisions at the time they make them. If you recently bought a personal computer or a car, you most likely experienced the difficulties of getting perfect information and making 'optimal' decisions in complex situations. As a result, you will probably not be surprised to find that there are serious flaws in the rational view of how managers make decisions. Nevertheless, the rational view is useful in providing a benchmark against which to compare actual managerial decision-making patterns.

In contrast to the rational view, several **non-rational models** of managerial decision making suggest that information-gathering and processing limitations make it difficult for managers to make optimal decisions. Within the non-rational framework, researchers have identified three main models of decision making: the Satisficing model, the Incremental model, and the Garbage Can model.

B **The Satisficing Model** During the 1950s economist Herbert Simon began to study the actual behaviours of managerial decision makers. On the basis of his studies, Simon offered the idea of bounded rationality as a framework through which actual managerial decision making can be better understood. 'Bounded rationality' means that the ability of managers to be perfectly rational in making decisions is limited by such factors as intelligence and time limits. The model suggests that the following factors commonly limit the degree to which managers are perfectly rational in making decisions:

- Decision makers may not have enough information, not only about the type of issue to be decided but also about possible alternatives and their strengths and limitations.
- Time and cost factors often limit the amount of information that can be gathered in regard to a particular decision.
- Decision makers' views about the relative importance of various pieces of data may cause them to overlook or ignore important information.
- The part of human memory that is used in making decisions can hold only a small amount of information at one time.
- The calculating capacities connected with intelligence limit the ability of decision makers to make optimal decisions, even if perfect information has been gathered.

Rather than optimizing their decisions, Simon argued, managers follow the Satisficing model, which says that managers look for alternatives only until they find one that looks satisfactory. This can be a good decision-making approach when the cost of delaying a decision or searching for a better alternative is greater than the reward from following such an approach. For example, if one is driving on an unfamiliar highway with only a little bit of gas left, it might be better to choose a gas station within sight than to hold out for one's favourite brand. On the other hand, managers sometimes make a habit of using the over-simple satisficing approach even in situations where the cost of searching for further alternatives is justified given the possible gain.

C **The Incremental Model** Another approach to decision making is the Incremental model, which says that managers make the smallest response possible that will reduce the problem to at least a manageable level. This approach is aimed more at short-term easing of a problem than toward making decisions that will help achieve long-term goals. Like the Satisficing model, the Incremental model does not require that managers process a great deal of information in order to take action. One researcher compared this model to the actions of a homeowner who deals with the problem of not enough electric power points by using extension cables. In the long run, the homeowner's incremental decisions may prove not to work, since additional pieces of electrical equipment may cause fuses to blow.

D **The Garbage Can Model** The Garbage Can model of decision making says that managers behave in an almost random pattern in making non-programmed decisions. In other words, decision outcomes happen by chance, depending on such factors as the people who happen to be involved, the problems that they happen to be concerned with at the time, the opportunities that they happen to find, and the favorite solutions that they happen to prefer. The Garbage Can strategy is most likely to be used when managers have no goal preferences, the means of achieving goals are unclear, and/or decision-makers change rapidly. Desirable outcomes can sometimes be achieved with a Garbage Can strategy, but this approach can also lead to serious difficulties. For example, Gould, Inc. was once a $2 billion maker of computers and other electronic equipment. However, the company ran into problems when its 'iron-willed' CEO, William Ylvisaker, decided to remake the company by investing in Florida real estate and other endeavours that did not fit a reasonably defined strategy. Finally, the company was taken over by Japan-based Nippon Mining after Nippon made a $1.1 billion offer for what was left of Gould. Thus, while the Garbage Can approach can sometimes lead managers to take advantage of unforeseen opportunities, it can also lead to severe problems from which it may be difficult to recover.

110

Source: K Bartol & DC Martin, *Management*, Irwin/ McGraw-Hill America 1998, pp.142–144

Business vocabulary

The most common collocation pattern in many academic texts is adjective–noun. The key terms from the text that are focused on in this lesson are all adjective–noun collocations.

A | Decision-making

1 Look back at paragraph A in the text on page 29. Check you understand decision-making terms a–f. Match them to definitions 1–6.

a economic theory (line 3) ____

b economic behaviour (line 4) ____

c optimal decision (line 11) ____

d complex situation (line 17) ____

e serious flaw (line 18) ____

f decision-making pattern (line 22) ____

1 an idea linked to money, trade, finance or industry
2 a complicated state or condition
3 a major fault, failing or limitation
4 the best choice, conclusion or judgement
5 actions or performance related to, e.g. money or trade
6 a system or picture of how choices are made

2 Choose a phrase from 1 a–f to complete the summary below. Use the plural form if necessary.

Managers often have to make decisions in
¹_____ , and in an ideal world they would make ²_____ . It was felt in the past that the best decisions could be made based on ³_____ with an understanding of the ⁴_____ of the company. However, this theory had ⁵_____ , because managers often do not know all the information to make a truly rational decision. In many cases, ⁶_____ are not rational or logical, indeed some theorists would argue that they are completely random.

B | Adjective–noun collocations

1 Look at paragraphs B–D on page 29. Find adjective–noun collocations that match definitions 1–6.

1 re _ _ ti _ _ im _ _ _ _ an _ _ (para. **B**)
the significance of something in relation to something else

2 p _ _ _ ib _ _ g _ _ n (para. **B**)
a potential increase or achievement

3 l _ _ g-t _ _ _ g _ _ _ s (para. **C**)
aims that are far in the future

4 r _ _ d _ _ p _ _ _ e _ _ (para. **D**)
a way that is without logic or order

5 de _ _ _ abl _ o _ _ _ om _ (para. **D**)
a target or result that would be ideal in a given situation

6 d _ _ _ n _ _ st _ _ _ e _ _ (para. **D**)
a plan, often related to a business or organization, that is clearly set out

2 Complete a–f with the correct form of a phrase in 1.

a The company had a clearly _____ for entering new markets and establishing their position.

b Decisions taken in isolation are often weak, as they need to be seen in terms of _____ to each other.

c The _____ were significant, considering how small the investment was.

d The most _____ of the merger would be for both companies to save money, grow in strength and become the market leader within the field.

e It is often felt that bonuses awarded in companies reward immediate performance but do not encourage a focus on _____ or encourage a strategy that would secure a company's future.

f Much economic theory is based on logic and order, which many would argue is opposed to the reality of _____ of behaviour.

Writing skills

Brainstorming is the first step towards developing ideas for a piece of writing. It means to think of quickly and write down notes, questions, and ideas related to a topic. It forms the basis for organizing your ideas and developing research questions.

A | Developing ideas

1 Look at the list of brainstormed ideas about the theory of 'Rational decision-making' from the text on page 29. Which ideas are connected?

2 Choose another decision-making model from the text. Spend two or three minutes writing down a list of your ideas related to this model.

3 Compare in pairs. Put all your ideas into one list. Cross out any ideas that are the same.

4 Which ideas are from the text? Are there extra ideas?

B | Organizing ideas

1 In pairs, look at the 'ideas map' of the brainstorm in A1.

  a Where is the main topic?

  b What are the three main groupings?

  c Which ideas are from the reading text? Which are extra ideas?

2 Would you organize the ideas about 'Rational decision-making' in A1 differently? Discuss in pairs.

3 Use your brainstormed ideas list about another decision-making model from the text on page 29. Create your own 'mind map' for the theory.

Research task

Research a different decision-making theory or case study. Develop your ideas and organize them using the brainstorming and mapping techniques. Be prepared to use your ideas map to talk about your research findings.

Rational decision-making

When – 1st half 20C
Why was it popular? – managers supposed to be good at job of decision-making
Which economic theory was it based on?
Describe model – optimal decisions
Optimal for whom? (individual, dept, company ...)
All information available, e.g. price, performance, speed, needs
How are decisions made? Factors involved include price, performance, speed, capability, etc.
Problems with model – not how managers make decisions
Complex situations – not good
Personal bias of manager / self-interest, other ...
Company aims not always economic > social, ethical?
Understanding lots of information – hard to process
Getting information
Information hard to find
Information not available

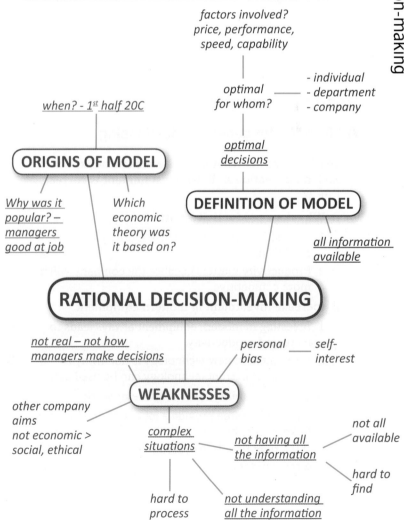

8 Increasing productivity

Study focus

1 **What is the difference between 'productivity' and 'performance'? Explain to a partner.**

2 **Have you ever had a job where your productivity or your performance was assessed? Tell a partner about**

  • your role in the company or workplace.
  • how you were assessed.

3 **In which of these jobs do you think it is easiest to assess productivity and performance? Think of one way to assess these things for each job.**

	Productivity	Performance
librarian		
production line worker		
sales representative		
teacher		

Reading strategies

A | Reading for general understanding

Read the extract from an academic textbook. For each main section A–E, which statement is correct, 1 or 2?

A Why does productivity matter?
 1 Productivity matters because more units can be produced.
 2 Productivity matters because the company will be more competitive.

B Increase investment in modern equipment
 1 Investing in modern equipment always leads to increased productivity.
 2 Investment in new technology is not always needed, as current technology can be used better.

C Improve the ability level of those at work
 1 Companies often provide a lot of training in order to keep their best staff.
 2 If the right people are recruited, training is not always needed.

D Improve employee motivation
 1 People often do not want to work hard.
 2 Business performance is not affected by individual motivation.

E The role of management
 1 Long-term productivity is the main focus of most managers.
 2 Meeting short-term demands is the main focus of most managers.

B | Reading closely for detailed information

Read the text again and answer the questions about sections A–E.

A Why does productivity matter?
 1 Which factory is more productive?
 2 What two pricing strategies could they use?

B Increase investment in modern equipment
 3 Why was General Motors technological investment not successful?
 4 How can a company improve productivity from existing equipment?

C Improve the ability level of those at work
 5 What benefits are there from training staff?
 6 What is the negative short-run impact for a company?

D Improve employee motivation
 7 What does Herzberg feel is the key to success in a company?
 8 What does the phrase 'both cases' refer to?

E The role of management
 9 How can managers improve the productivity of a firm?
 10 What was the aim of Komatsu?

C | Reacting to the text

Discuss in pairs.

 • What are the four methods of improving productivity mentioned in the text?
 • Which method of improving productivity do you think is the most effective?
 • Could you use all these methods in any job?

Productivity and performance

Why does productivity matter?

A The output per employee is a very important measure of a firm's performance. It has a direct impact on the cost of producing a unit. If productivity increases, then, assuming wages are unchanged, the labour cost per unit
5 will fall. Imagine that in one factory employees make 5 pairs of shoes a day but in another one they make 10 pairs per day. Assuming the wage rate is the same this means the labour cost of a pair of shoes will be halved in the second factory. With lower labour costs this firm is
10 likely to be in a better competitive position.

   a By increasing productivity a firm can improve its competitiveness. <u>It</u> can either sell its products at a lower price or keep the price as <u>it</u> was and enjoy a higher profit margin. This is why firms continually
15 monitor their productivity relative to their competitors and, where possible, try to increase it. However, they need to make sure that quality does not suffer in the rush to produce more. It may be necessary to set both productivity and quality targets.

How to increase productivity

B Increase investment in modern equipment

20 With more modern or more sophisticated machines and better production processes, output per worker should improve. Many modern factories have very few production workers. Mechanisation and automation are everywhere. However, firms face financial
25 constraints and should be cautious about assuming that mechanisation guarantees higher profits. **b** In the 1980s American car giant General Motors invested billions of dollars in robotic production lines. Breakdowns meant <u>they</u> never proved as efficient as
30 intended. More importantly, when customer buying habits switched to smaller cars, the machines proved much less flexible than humans. The investment proved unprofitable and by the early 1990s the company was close to financial failure.

35   It is also true to say that many people call for new technology when in fact more output can be squeezed out of existing equipment. It may prove more efficient to run the machines for longer, spend more on careful maintenance to prevent breakdowns and discuss how
40 to improve working practices. **c** Firms can often achieve significant productivity gains without new equipment. <u>This</u> is the reason for the success of the *kaizen* approach taken in many firms. Important benefits can be achieved from what seems like relatively small changes
45 to the way the firm operates rather than large-scale investment in technology.

C Improve the ability level of those at work

To increase productivity a firm may need to introduce more training for its employees. A skilled and well-trained workforce is likely to produce more and
50 make fewer mistakes. Employees should be able to complete the task more quickly and not need as much supervision or advice. They should be able to solve their own work-related problems and may be in a better position to contribute ideas on how to increase
55 productivity further.

   However, firms are often reluctant to invest in training because employees may leave and work for another firm once they have gained more skills. Training also involves higher costs in the short run,
60 which the business may not be able to afford, and the actual training period may cause disruptions to the normal flow of work. There is also a danger that the training will not provide sufficient gains to justify the initial investment. So any spending in this area
65 needs to be properly costed and researched. Simply training people for the sake of it is obviously of limited value. However, in general, UK firms do not have a particularly good record in training. More investment here could probably have a significant effect on the
70 UK's productivity levels.

   It should also be remembered that elaborate training may not be necessary for a firm which recruits the right people. Great care must be taken in the selection process to find staff with the right skills and attitudes. A firm
75 with a good reputation locally will find it much easier to pick the best people. This is why many firms take great care over their relations with the local community.

D Improve employee motivation

d Professor Herzberg once said that most people's idea of a fair day's work was less than half what <u>they</u> could
80 give. If they wanted to. The key to success, he felt, was to create the circumstances in which people wanted to give all they could to the job. There is no doubt that motivation matters. A motivated salesforce may achieve twice the sales levels of an unmotivated one. A
85 motivated computer technician may correct twice the computer faults of an unmotivated one. And, in both cases, overall business performance will be affected.

E The role of management

The management's style and ability can have a significant impact on motivation and on how effectively
90 resources are used. Good managers can bring about substantial productivity gains through well-organised work, the effective management of people and the coordination of resources. Bad managers can lead to wastage, inefficiency and low productivity.

95   Perhaps the key management role is to identify increasing productivity as a permanent objective. For

example, the Japanese bulldozer company Komatsu set a target of a 10% productivity increase every year, until the world-leading American producer Caterpillar

100 had been overhauled. In many firms, productivity is not a direct target. The focus, day by day, is on production not productivity. After all, it is production which ensures customer orders are fulfilled. An operations manager, faced with a 10% increase in orders, may simply ask

105 the workforce to do overtime. The work gets done; the workforce is happy to earn extra money; and it's all rather easy to do. Harder by far to reorganise the workplace to make production more effective. Managers whose main focus is on the short term, therefore, think

110 of production not productivity.

Source: I Marcouse, B Martin, M Surridge & N Wall, *Business studies*, Hodder Arnold 2003, pp.211–214

Glossary

suffer (line 17): (v) get worse

kaizen (line 42): (n) Japanese method of running a company by always looking to improve ways of working

for the sake of it (line 66): (expression) with no specific purpose in mind

bulldozer (line 97): (n) heavy vehicle for pushing earth and stones

overhauled (line 100): (v) overtaken, beaten

Business vocabulary

A | Pronoun referents

Pronouns are frequently used to refer to other, usually earlier, ideas in a text. They help to avoid repetition of words. However, they can also make a text harder to follow. Recognizing pronoun referencing will help you to understand the progression of ideas and information in a text.

1 Look at the extract below from the text on page 33.

> The output per employee is a very important measure of a firm's performance. It has a direct impact on the cost of producing a unit. (lines 1–3)

  a Which word in the second sentence refers back to an idea in the first sentence?

  b Which idea does this word refer back to?

2 Look at highlighted sentences a–d in the text on page 33. Circle the idea that the <u>underlined</u> pronouns refer to.

3 Which other word in the paragraph below do pronouns 1–6 refer to?

Productivity is key to competitiveness; without [1] **it**, companies will struggle to maximize [2] **their** potential. [3] **It** impacts on the profitability of a company, and [4] **this** can have a direct impact on factors such as salaries or working conditions. Unfortunately, many employees do not look at [5] **it** in this way, and it is therefore the role of the manager to focus on [6] **this** aspect of the business.

B | 'Production' or 'productivity'?

1 Write an exact definition of the difference between 'production' and 'productivity'.

Production is …

Productivity is …

2 Complete sentences a–e with 'production' or 'productivity'.

  a There was an increase in _____ from 10 items per hour to 12 items per hour.

  b Increasing _____ means not only producing more but being more efficient.

  c The monthly _____ target was easily met.

  d Working on a _____ line is a very repetitive job.

  e Decreases in _____ can mean a company is less competitive.

3 In pairs, choose the correct option.

  a The increase in *production / productivity* cut costs by 20%.

  b The *actions / activities* required to do a job make up a job description.

  c He was praised for his great *sensitivity / sensation*.

  d The computer is one of the greatest *creativity / creations* of the last century.

4 Explain the meaning of the words you didn't use in sentences a–d in 3. Write four sentences using the words.

Writing skills

Two methods for supporting a main idea are
1) giving a reason, and 2) giving an example. These
support the main idea by **either** showing why the
opinion is held, **or** giving an example to illustrate
the main point. Sometimes **both** are used together
to give extra support to a main idea. It is useful to
learn the kinds of expressions that are used to show
more clearly that a reason or example is being given.

A | Expanding an idea with reasons and examples

1 Look at extracts 1 and 2 from the text on page 33.

> 1 The output per employee is a very important measure of a firm's performance. It has a direct impact on the cost of producing a unit. (lines 1–3)

> 2 By increasing productivity a firm can improve its competitiveness. It can either sell its products at a lower price or keep the price as it was and enjoy a higher profit margin. (lines 11–14)

   a Underline the main idea in each extract.
   b Is the main idea in each case supported by a reason or an example?

2 Complete sentences a and b with either *for example* or *because*.

   a The output per employee is a very important measure of a firm's performance _____ it has a direct impact on the cost of producing a unit.
   b By increasing productivity a firm can improve its competitiveness. _____ , it can either sell its products at a lower price or keep the price as it was and enjoy a higher profit margin.

3 How are sentences a and b in 2 different from the extracts in 1?

4 Which of the expressions in the list are used to give an example? Which are used to give a reason?

as a result of	because
by way of illustration	due to (the fact that)*
for instance	in the case of
… shows this point clearly	since
such as	

* Note due to + noun (*Staff were made redundant,* **due to** *the economic downturn.*) BUT *due to the fact that* + verb phrase (*Staff were made redundant,* **due to the fact that** *there was an economic downturn.*)

5 Complete sentences a–e with a phrase from 4.

   a Training staff can have a number of positive effects, _____ , employees may be able to suggest methods to improve productivity.
   b Companies are not always keen to invest in staff development, _____ the fact that staff may leave for another company.
   c Investment in technology is not always guaranteed to increase productivity. General Motors _____ .
   d Training is expensive in the short run and, _____ this, many companies choose not to invest in staff development.
   e Issues _____ short-term production targets often mean that a company does not operate productively. _____ , a company with a 10% increase in orders may simply ask people to work more overtime.

6 Look at a–e in 5 again. When are full stops and commas used? Which expressions come at the beginning, in the middle and/or at the end of a sentence?

B | Writing practice

Look at sentences 1–4. Provide one example and one reason for each. Use a range of expressions and correct punctuation.

For a company to be competitive it needs to be productive, because …

> … *increased productivity can lead to a reduction in the costs of production.*

For a company to be competitive it needs to be productive. For example …

> … *a company that can produce the same at costs lower than its rivals is likely to be more competitive.*

1 Many people are only willing to give half of what they are capable of giving …
2 Motivation is important in the performance of a business …
3 Management style and ability can have an impact on the productivity of a firm …
4 Staff performance needs to be evaluated …

Research task

Research one company that has increased productivity. What methods did they use? Give reasons why the method was used, and examples of how it was used.

9 Job satisfaction

Study focus

1 List five factors that are important to you in a work environment, e.g. your own desk.

2 Compare your lists in pairs.
   - Agree on your top five.
   - Rank your top five in order from 'most important' to 'least important'.

Reading strategies

A | Reading quickly for specific information

1 In pairs, read two extracts from an academic textbook. Answer the questions as quickly as you can.

   Student A, read paragraph B, 'Dimensions of job satisfaction'.

   a How many dimensions of job satisfaction are there?
   b Which factors are each of the following linked to?

   1 education and qualifications _____ factors
   2 economic, social and governmental _____ factors
   3 attitudes, beliefs and values _____ factors
   4 relationships with co-workers _____ factors
   5 size and structure of company _____ factors

   Student B, read paragraph D, 'Alienation at work'.

   c How many dimensions of alienation at work are there?
   d Which dimension is each of the following linked to?

   1 a lack of purpose in work _____
   2 a lack of control over work _____
   3 work is not a central life issue _____
   4 not integrated into the work group _____

2 Explain to your partner what you found out in your section.

B | Identifying point of view

1 Read the whole text quickly. Match the names to their contribution to the text a–c.

   the Chartered Management Institute ___
   Charles Handy ___
   LJ Mullins ___

   a the author of the text
   b a management expert quoted by the author
   c an organization who commissioned a study into working environments

2 Look at opinions a–d. Then read paragraphs A and C again. Who expresses each opinion: Handy, Mullins or the CMI study?

   a Defining job satisfaction is challenging. (para. **A**)
   b The buildings and facilities people work with impact on job satisfaction. (para. **C**)
   c Poor office space can have a negative impact on clients. (para. **C**)
   d People would give up salary for a better office. (para. **C**)

3 Tick the opinions each person would agree with, according to the text.

   a **Marx** would agree that employees …

   1 should be separated from their role. ___
   2 need a satisfying role. ___

   b **Blauner** would agree that employees …

   1 shouldn't be concerned with work processes. ___
   2 should be concerned with the purpose of work. ___
   3 need to be part of a team. ___
   4 do not want work to be a central life issue. ___

C | Reacting to the text

1 Which statements do you agree with and why?

   a Job satisfaction is necessary in order to achieve a high level of motivation and performance.
   b Satisfaction leads to performance.
   c Performance leads to satisfaction.

2 Answer about your own experiences of work.
   - Have you ever been dissatisfied in a job? If so which dimension in the text was it most linked to?
   - Have you ever felt alienated at work? If so which dimension in the text was it most closely linked to?

The meaning and nature of job satisfaction

A Attempting to understand the nature of job satisfaction and its effects on work performance is not easy. Job satisfaction is a complex and multi-faceted concept, which can mean different things to different people. It
5 is usually linked with motivation, but the nature of this relationship is not clear. Satisfaction is not the same as motivation. Job satisfaction is more of an attitude, an internal state. It could, for example, be associated with a personal feeling of achievement, either quantitative
10 or qualitative.

Dimensions of job satisfaction

B There is some doubt whether job satisfaction consists of a single dimension or a number of separate dimensions. Some workers may be satisfied with certain aspects of their work and dissatisfied with other
15 aspects. Job satisfaction is itself a complex concept and difficult to measure objectively. The level of job satisfaction is affected by a wide range of variables relating to individual, social, cultural, organisational and environmental factors.

20 • **Individual factors** include personality, education and qualifications, intelligence and abilities, age, marital status, orientation to work.
• **Social factors** include relationships with co-workers, group working and norms, opportunities for
25 interaction, informal organisation.
• **Cultural factors** include underlying attitudes, beliefs and values.
• **Organisational factors** include nature and size, formal structure, HR policies and procedures,
30 employee relations, nature of the work, technology and work organisation, supervision and styles of leadership, management systems, working conditions.
• **Environmental factors** include economic, social, technical and governmental influences.

35 These different factors all affect the job satisfaction of certain individuals in a given set of circumstances but not necessarily in others.

C **The work environment** An increasingly important issue affecting job satisfaction and efficiency is the
40 nature of the work environment and workplace facilities. Handy argues that an inspired workplace will result in inspired workers and draws attention to the importance for work performance of the atmosphere, quality and style of buildings and offices. A 2003 study
45 by the Chartered Management Institute reports on UK managers' attitudes to and experiences of their physical working environment. The study was undertaken among a random sample of 4,000 managers across all levels and sectors and size of organisation. Topics
50 addressed included hours worked, commuting and travel, flexible working, the existing and preferred layout of offices and the use of new technologies. Concerns were expressed about the need for more quiet areas, under-equipped meeting rooms, lack of
55 adequate meeting space, and their offices not making a good impression on clients and visitors. Nearly half of those surveyed would relinquish one week's annual leave for a better office and sizable numbers would forgo £1,000 in salary or private medical insurance for
60 a significantly upgraded workspace. And even if the role, salary and benefits were no better, 45 per cent would contemplate changing companies in return for an improved work environment.

D **Alienation at work** One main approach to job
65 satisfaction is in terms of frustration and alienation at work. Job satisfaction can be seen as the obverse of frustration at work (discussed above). Alienation refers to the detachment of the person from their work role. The concept of alienation at work is associated
70 originally with the views of Marx. He saw the division of labour in pursuit of profit, and exploitation by employers, as a denial of the workers' need for self-expression. Workers became separated from the product of their work. Work no longer provided a
75 satisfying experience in itself, but represented a means of satisfying other external demands. The concept of alienation has been extended by Blauner. He describes alienation in terms of four dimensions: powerlessness, meaninglessness, isolation and self-estrangement.

80 • **Powerlessness** denotes the workers' lack of control over management policy, immediate work processes, or conditions of employment.
• **Meaninglessness** stems from standardisation and division of labour. It denotes the inability to see the
85 purpose of work done or to identify with the total production process or finished product.
• **Isolation** is not belonging to an integrated work group or to the social work organisation and not being guided by group norms of behaviour.
90 • **Self-estrangement** is the failure to see work as an end in itself or as a central life issue. Workers experience a depersonalised detachment and work is seen solely as a means to an end.

In recent years attention to job satisfaction has
95 also become more closely associated with broader approaches to improved job design and work organisation, and the quality of working life movement, and with stress and work/life balance.

Source: LJ Mullins, *Management and Organisational Behaviour,* Pearson, Harlow, 2007, pp.277–279

Glossary

multi-faceted (line 3): (adj) having many different parts
relinquish (line 57): (v) give up
contemplate (line 62): (v) consider, think about
obverse (line 66): (n) the other side of something

Business vocabulary

A | Research and data

The following words are all associated with types of data, the collection of data and the reporting of findings.

1 When conducting research, what different types of data can you collect? Complete the words.

   a q _ _ _ tit _ _ _ _ e
   b q _ _ _ ita _ _ _ e

2 Match the words in 1 to definitions 1 and 2.

   1 data related to something that can be measured
   2 data related to something that is not countable

3 Which type of data from 1 is being reported in this section of the text on page 37? Explain your reasons.

> Nearly half of those surveyed would relinquish one week's annual leave for a better office and sizable numbers would forgo £1,000 in salary or private medical insurance for a significantly upgraded workspace. (lines 56–60)

4 Read the sentence from the text.

> Job satisfaction is itself a complex concept and difficult to measure **objectively**. (lines 15–16)

Tick the best definition of *objectively*.

   a a judgement based on facts   ____
   b a judgement based on feelings and beliefs   ____

5 *subjective* is the opposite of *objective*. Tick the subjective opinion, 1 or 2.

> 1   Handy argues that an inspired workplace will result in inspired workers and draws attention to the importance for work performance of atmosphere, quality and style of buildings and offices. (lines 41–44)   ____

> 2   And even if the role, salary and benefits were no better, 45 per cent would contemplate changing companies in return for an improved work environment. (lines 60–63)   ____

6 Replace the phrases in *italics* in a–f with expressions from the list.

   an interview   to investigate   a questionnaire
   a random sample   to survey   to undertake

   a He agreed *to do* research into alienation at work.
   b They set out *to ask* 50 people about their opinion.
   c *A survey* was used to gather data from many people.
   d Qualitative in-depth data was important, so *a one-to-one discussion* was held.
   e The purpose of the research was *to look into* the main causes of dissatisfaction.
   f *An unplanned selection* of people was used in the study.

B | Connection and relationship

1 Read definitions a–h, and match the verbs in bold with prepositions from the list.

   by   from   in   of   to   with

   a indicating a connection between things:
      to be associated _____
   b to be made up of different parts:
      to consist _____
   c something has impacted on something else:
      to be affected _____
   d something is concerned with something else:
      relating _____
   e to happen because of something:
      to result _____
   f a way of doing something:
      an/the approach _____
   g to mention or speak about something:
      to refer _____
   h indicating the origins of something:
      to stem _____

2 Choose the correct option.

   a Job satisfaction is *associated with* / *consists of* work-life balance.
   b Job satisfaction *results in* / *consists of* five factors.
   c One *refer to* / *approach to* job satisfaction is focusing on the opposite, looking at 'dissatisfaction'.
   d Job satisfaction can be negatively *stemmed from* / *affected by* a feeling of isolation.
   e Powerlessness *approaches to* / *stems from* a feeling of a lack of control.
   f There are four dimensions *relating to* / *consisting of* alienation at work.
   g A lack of job satisfaction can *result in* / *refer to* poor worker performance.
   h 'Job satisfaction' *refers to* / *results in* an attitude or state.

Writing skills

A | Referencing and citation

Using information from your reading in your writing is a good way of improving your argument. It demonstrates your knowledge about a topic, and helps to support and strengthen any opinions you state. It is important to reference source material, and there are a number of methods; this lesson will focus on the Harvard system.

1 Look at the paragraph and answer the questions.

> Job satisfaction and the state of the workplace are seen to have an impact on employee productivity. According to Handy (1997), work performance is closely linked to the quality of the workplace. For example, by providing a well-equipped, modern, comfortable office environment that employees feel happy in, a company could make a positive impact on the job satisfaction of staff.

  a Underline the part of the paragraph that is the idea of Handy.
  b What information about the source is provided?
  c How does this strengthen the main point?

2 Look at the paragraph and answer the questions.

> 'Job satisfaction' is difficult to define, as it can mean many different things to different people. Mullins (2007:277) argues that job satisfaction is not one single thing, but 'a wide range of variables relating to individual, social, cultural, organisational and environmental factors.' Clearly, these factors will be different in different contexts, companies, cultures and between individuals. Therefore, an exact definition is difficult to provide.

  a Underline the part of the paragraph that is the idea of Mullins.
  b What information about the source is provided?
  c How does this strengthen the main point?

3 The extract in 2 uses a direct quotation.
  a Which of the following defines a direct quotation?
    1 It uses the exact words of the author.
    2 It uses the ideas of the author but expressed in original words.
  b How are the words of the author shown?
  c When do you think it might be better to use a direct quote?

4 Look at sentences 1–3 that refer to sourced ideas. Underline the three reporting verbs.
  1 Johnson (1999) claims that job satisfaction is easily measured.
  2 Kingston (2010) states that job satisfaction consists of five dimensions.
  3 Jameson (2008) demonstrates that the working environment plays a key role in job satisfaction.

5 If you used the sourced ideas from 4 in your writing, which reporting verb would help to show that …
  a you are probably using the author's idea to support your own argument?
  b the author's idea is neutral in relation to your own argument?
  c you are probably disagreeing with the author's idea in relation to your own argument?

6 Put the verbs in the list into three groups which suggest that a sourced idea is either Neutral, For or Against another argument.

  acknowledges asserts cautions contends defines
  describes disputes maintains states

Neutral	For	Against

B | Writing practice

The text on page 37, 'The meaning and nature of job satisfaction', is sourced from:

> LJ Mullins, *Management and Organisational Behaviour*, Pearson, Harlow, 2007, pp.277–279

1 Use paragraph B of the text and the source information above to write a direct quotation to support this statement:

'Workers may not be satisfied with all aspects of their job.'

2 Use paragraph D of the text and the source information above to write an indirect quotation to support this statement:

'The analysis of job satisfaction has changed in recent years.'

Research task

Find a study looking into the area of job satisfaction. What area of job satisfaction does the study look at? What were the conclusions of the study?

10 New business

Study focus

1 If you could start any business of your own, what would it be and why? Tell a partner.

2 Brainstorm at least three positive and three negative ideas about starting a business.

Reading strategies

A | Reading quickly for general understanding

1 Quickly read the extract about new businesses from an academic textbook. Which statement, a, b or c, best completes a summary of the text?

The text describes …
a the number of small businesses started every year.
b the challenges a business faces in surviving beyond the first years.
c the main challenges faced by the manufacturing sector.

2 Identify the introduction, the conclusion and the main part of the text.

3 The main part of the text describes factors that affect the survival rate of companies. Match factors 1–6 to explanations a–f.

1 Minimum efficient scale ___
2 The start-up size of firm ___
3 The overall rate of innovation in the firm's industry ___
4 The rate of innovation among small firms in the firm's industry ___
5 The growth rate of the industry ___
6 Whether the firm is a multi-plant operation ___

a the number of locations of operation
b the speed that the sector is expanding
c the smallest size at which a company or plant can be cost-effective
d the number of new ideas normally current within the sector
e the number of new ideas of small businesses within the sector
f how big a firm is at the beginning

B | Understanding main and supporting ideas

1 Read the introduction again. Tick the main idea.

a Many companies are registered every year. ___
b Many new companies fail to survive. ___
c Many companies have short-term plans. ___

2 Look at statements a–f about new companies. Match what happened to factors 1–6 in the text.

a 'The market was continually expanding, which meant that there was enough business for everybody, and nobody was really in strong competition with each other.' ___

b 'Some of the other companies in the market were so large compared to us that we just could not produce the same amounts at the same price.' ___

c 'So many new ideas were coming out that it was difficult to compete.' ___

d 'It was very easy to develop new ideas in the field, so almost any company could do so. We faced so much competition from other small companies we just couldn't compete.' ___

e 'We thought it would be a good idea to have a number of distribution centres around the country, but in hindsight we should have had one central location.' ___

f 'We were so small when we started we just couldn't compete on costs.' ___

3 Read the conclusion again. Tick the main idea.

a New companies should probably not try to start. ___
b New companies need to ask a number of questions before starting. ___
c New companies are unlikely to succeed. ___

C | Reacting to the text

1 Think back to the business you said you would like to start in *Study focus*. How might these questions impact on your business idea?

• Is the industry a fast-moving one technologically?
• How rapidly is the industry growing?
• How likely is the entry to provoke retaliation from existing firms in the sector who face a potential drop in sales?

2 How risky do you think your business idea is?

Survival and growth

A Less than 50 per cent of businesses registered for VAT in the United Kingdom are still registered six years later and a similar percentage applies to registrations of companies. Company registration data also provide
5 some information on survival over the much longer term. They show that only 11 per cent of companies registered in 1950–4 were still registered in March 2004, and that the percentage for those registered in the period 1900–9 was less than five (Department
10 of Trade and Industry 2004a:35). Thus nearly all companies have gone within a century. Why do so many firms exit so soon after entry? Some people who set up in business may *intend* only to stay for a very short period. But probably for the majority of those who
15 exit, their failure is, for them, early.

B The fact that the overall exit rate is high among young businesses is consistent with the systematic explanation of why some businesses survive and others do not. This has been comprehensively explored in an
20 excellent study by Audretsch (1995). He found, for his sample of 11,000 manufacturing businesses set up in 1976, that the likelihood of their survival to 1986 was affected by the following.

1 Minimum efficient scale (MES). The higher the
25 MES at plant level, the lower the chances of survival. The rationale for this finding is not difficult to find. For any given initial size, the larger the MES, the bigger the cost disadvantage faced by the entrant. MES is not easily measured, but Audretsch (1995) uses a measure
30 widely adopted elsewhere, the mean size of the largest plants in the firm's industry which account for 50 per cent of the output.

2 The start-up size of firm. The larger the firm's own initial size is, the lower the cost disadvantage it has
35 to overcome, and thus the higher are its chances of survival.

3 The overall rate of innovation in the firm's industry. The higher this rate, the greater the uncertainty faced by the entrant, and thus the higher
40 the rate of exit.

4 The rate of innovation among small firms in the firm's industry. The argument in (3) applies even more for small, technologically innovative firms. Winter (1984), drawing on Schumpeter, distinguishes between
45 an 'entrepreneurial' regime which is more favourable to innovation by entrants and less favourable to innovation by established firms, and a 'routinised' regime where the reverse is true. New entry is likely to be higher in the former, but the survival rate is

50 likely to be lower, due to the fact that relatively more firms will be engaged in innovative activity, with all its uncertainties. In routinised regimes, on the other hand, new entrants are much less likely to enter the industry on the basis of an innovation, and will thus have a
55 lower probability of exit. The particular measure used by Audretsch (1995) was the number of innovations in firms with fewer than 500 employees divided by the total number of employees in such firms. It is not known how sensitive these results are to the particular
60 measure used.

5 The growth rate of the industry. Audretsch (1995) argues that the higher this growth rate, the greater the chances of survival. One reason for this is that growth tends to be positively associated with profitability, and
65 as a result, incumbent firms will be less likely to take retaliatory action against new entrants. A growing industry will also mean that entrants can come in without taking sales from existing businesses.

6 Whether the firm is a multi-plant operation.
70 Where a firm has more than one plant, its overall employment size will be a poor measure of the average employment size of its constituent plants. The gap between MES and the size of individual plants will thus *appear* to be less than it really is. It would be
75 expected that, because of this overstatement, a multi-plant firm would be less likely (other things being equal) to survive.

C These findings highlight the importance of underlying economic influences in determining survival. New
80 entrants ignore these factors at their own risk. Audretsch's (1995) study also provides ideas for appropriate questions that a would-be small business owner might ask prior to setting up. For example, at what size will it be possible to compete in costs terms
85 with rivals? Is the industry, both generally and in relation to small business in particular, a fast moving one technologically and what are the risks associated with entering that environment? How rapidly is the industry growing? How likely is the entry to provoke
90 retaliation from existing firms who face a potential drop in sales?

Source: P Johnson, *The economics of small firms*, Routledge 2007, pp.64–68

Glossary

incumbent (line 65): (adj) currently in place
retaliatory (line 66): (adj) attacking back

Business vocabulary

A | Challenge

The following expressions describe how challenges impact on individuals and how they cope with them.

1 Look at the two phrases in *italics* from the text on page 41. Explain the difference between *to be affected by* (*a problem*) and *to overcome* (*a problem*).

> **a** He found, for his sample of 11,000 manufacturing businesses set up in 1976, that the likelihood of their survival to 1986 *was affected by* the following. (lines 20–23)

> **b** The larger the firm's own initial size is, the lower the cost disadvantage it has to *overcome*, and thus the higher are its chances of survival. (lines 33–36)

2 Put the 'challenge' expressions in the list into two groups of similar meaning.

to be affected by	to be confronted by	to deal with
to be faced by	to overcome	to rise above
to tackle	to be threatened by	

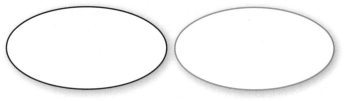

3 Compare your two groups in pairs. Explain how you have divided them.

4 Match expressions a–c to other expressions from 2 with the most similar meaning.

  a to deal with   _____

  b to be faced by   _____

  c to overcome   _____

5 Which expressions from 2 could replace the phrases in *italics* in a and b?

  a The company *were influenced by* other competitors in the market.

  b The project *was put at risk by* the changes in the sector.

6 Write three sentences combining two 'challenge' expressions, one from each group in 2.

> *The company **was affected by** its small size and had to **deal with** it by trying to increase rapidly.*

B | Measurements and amounts

The following expressions describe concepts of 'quantity'.

1 Match words a–h to definitions 1–8.

  a average   ____   **e** overall   ____

  b majority   ____   **f** percentage   ____

  c mean   ____   **g** proportion   ____

  d minority   ____   **h** sample   ____

  1 the largest part of a group of people or things

  2 including all things or people involved in a particular situation

  3 a part or share of a whole

  4 typical or normal

  5 the smallest part of a group of people or things

  6 the amount found by adding together all the numbers in a group and dividing the total by the number of numbers

  7 a number of people or things from a larger group used to represent the whole group

  8 the number, amount, or rate of something expressed as part of a total of 100

2 Complete sentences a–h with a word from 1. Sometimes more than one answer is possible.

  a A _____ of 1,000 companies showed that roughly 75% of all new businesses do not survive beyond five years.

  b The _____ length of time a company exists is three years.

  c The _____ small company typically needs to be very innovative.

  d The _____ size of the company is less important than the number of locations it operates in.

  e The _____ of small companies do not survive 100 years.

  f Only a _____ of companies survive 100 years.

  g The _____ of companies in the market that are able to innovate rapidly can affect the success of a new entrant.

  h The _____ of new companies that survive might increase if a company asks itself the right questions at the start.

3 Use words a–h from 1. Write five sentences describing:

companies   salaries   sectors

> *The **majority** of people work in the retail sector.*

Writing skills

A | Writing introductions and conclusions

Introductions typically move from general to specific. They indicate the overall structure of the piece of writing, and should include a clear statement about the main opinion or line of argument in the essay. This statement can be rephrased in the concluding paragraph of the essay to provide a link back to the main argument.

1 Put sentences a–d into the correct order, from GENERAL to SPECIFIC, to form an introduction.

a | The reasons for this are wide and varied, including factors such as size, innovation, location and efficiency.

b | Only one in five new companies in the UK survives beyond their first five years of trading.

c | However, this essay will argue that the main reason for failure is the large number of businesses that enter sectors that are no longer growing.

d | This rate has been consistent for a number of years now, and only four per cent of companies have actually existed for 100 years or more.

2 The sentence in an introduction that contains the main line of argument is sometimes called a 'thesis statement'. Which sentence in 1 is the thesis statement?

3 It is important that the opinion in a thesis statement is very clear. Which sentence a–c makes a good thesis statement?

a New businesses in the UK often fail.
b New businesses in particularly innovative sectors are at most risk of failure.
c Starting a new business has both advantages and disadvantages.

4 Tick the features you would *not* expect to find in a conclusion.

a statement of the main argument   ____
a link to the introduction   ____
a summary of the stages of the text   ____
new ideas or information   ____
a reference to the future   ____
questions for the reader to think about   ____

5 Look at the examples of rephrasing. Then rewrite sentences a–e so that they have a similar or complementary meaning. Change as many words as you can.

New <u>companies often fail</u>.
= New *firms are frequently unsuccessful.*

<u>Established</u> brands are <u>rarely innovative</u>.
= *Well-known* brands are *not often fresh or exciting.*

a Many developing economies are based on manufacturing goods.
b Most new businesses are internet companies.
c Very few new businesses survive beyond five years.
d Customer loyalty is key for all businesses but especially small businesses.
e Many companies fail because they do not understand the market well enough.

6 Rephrase thesis statements a–d so that you could use them in a conclusion.

Larger start-up companies are more likely to be successful than new small companies.

New companies that are small in size have less chance of success than large companies.

a Companies operating in multiple locations are faced by greater risk than those working in only one location.
b Entering a market where existing companies have a high level of efficiency poses a greater risk to new firms.
c Innovative sectors are likely to be more challenging to enter than non-innovative ones.
d A new company with a poor business plan is more likely to fail than one with a well-developed strategy.

B | Writing practice

1 Write an introduction for this essay topic. Remember to start from general and move to specific. Make sure you include a thesis statement.

New companies are highly unlikely to survive more than five years. Discuss.

2 Paraphrase your thesis statement from the introduction for use in a conclusion.

Research task

Research current market conditions relating to a new business. What type of business is it? What chance of success do you think this company has, and why? Write a thesis statement.

11 The impact of IT

Study focus

1 How many different things do you have that are run by a computer processor? In pairs, in one minute, list as many things as you can. Then compare with another pair. Which pair has the most?

2 Which things in 1 would be easiest to live without, and which would be hardest to live without? Discuss your ideas and reasons in pairs.

Reading strategies

A | Understanding a text using background knowledge

You are going to read an extract from an academic textbook written in 2007, about IT developments. Before you read …

1 List five technological changes that have happened in the last one hundred years.

2 Rank your list in 1 in order from 1 (biggest impact they have had on companies) to 5 (smallest impact). Compare in pairs.

3 Think of some examples of how these things have impacted on the way businesses operate.

4 In pairs, agree the differences between these terms.

Internet   intranet   extranet

5 Give at least one example of how companies can use each of the '…net' technologies in 4 to improve their business.

Now read 'The evolution of information systems'. Compare your ideas for 1–5 with the information in the text.

B | Reading closely for detailed information

According to the text, what are the most recent changes in each of these inventions?

1 the telephone
2 the television
3 the networked computer
4 the Internet

C | Understanding the relationship between text and graphic

1 Look at Figure 11.1 in the text, 'The widening effects of information systems'. Match the five stages in the figure to phrases a–e.

  a More business functions supported by information systems
  b Competitive use of information systems by innovating business processes
  c One business function supported by an information system
  d Joint information systems amongst organisations, e.g. by using the Internet
  e Information systems linked and integrated by joint databases

2 Read paragraph C.

  a Check your answers in 1.
  b What is the key difference between Stages 1–4 and Stage 5?

3 Look at Figure 11.2 in the text, 'Stages in using the Internet'. In pairs, think about how IT is used in businesses. Define the five terms to show the differences between them.

Information
Interaction
Transaction
Integration
Transformation

4 Read paragraph E.

  a Check your definitions of the five terms in 3. What extra information does the text provide?
  b Which term is not explained in the text? Can you explain it to your partner?

D | Reacting to the text

Discuss in pairs.

• What technological changes have happened since this article was written in 2007?
• What do you think will happen to traditional high street businesses as a result of the development of the Internet?

The evolution of information systems

Convergence of voice, vision and data

A The most dramatic changes in managing data, information and knowledge come from the rapid convergence of three technologies that developed independently during their long histories: the telephone
5 was invented in 1876, the first television transmission occurred in 1926, and the electronic computer goes back to 1946, if not earlier. For much of that time the pace of change was slow, but began to gather pace in the late 1980s. (Cairncross, 2001, p.27)

B **Major developments** include:
10 • *The telephone* The ability to send signals along glass fibre-optic cables has increased capacity, and reduced cost, dramatically. The cost of carrying additional calls is virtually zero, irrespective of distance. This has encouraged people to use the telephone not
15 only for speech, but for passing data and pictures between fixed computers and between them and the growing range of mobile devices. The cost of long-distance communication continues to fall, with major implications for managing businesses around the world.
20 • *The television* Although consumers rapidly adopted television after the launch of the first commercial station in 1947, the technology changed little for many years. A breakthrough came with the development of communications satellites, which enabled viewers to
25 see that they were in some respects part of a global community. The other big change was when broadcasters began to transmit programmes in digital form, increasing the capacity of available channels, and foreshadowing the convergence of televisions and computers.
30 • *The networked computer* By fitting more power into the microchips that are at the heart of a computer, engineers are able to roughly double computing power every two years. As the power of each microchip multiplies so the price of computing falls, leading to smaller
35 computers and greater capacity. From being stand-alone calculators, computers are now embedded in many other gadgets – such as games and video cameras.
• *The Internet* The invention of the Transmission Control Protocol/Internet Protocol (TCP/IP) provides a common
40 language and a set of rules that enable computers all over the world to talk to each other. TCP/IP does this by specifying the format in which data sent over the Internet must be packaged – enabling telephone, television and computer networks to connect with each
45 other as a single network. Linking mobile phones to the Internet has led to the explosive growth of the 'Wireless Internet', which in effect liberates the computer from the desktop, enabling information to pass readily between people wherever they are.

C Figure 11.1 shows the widening role of information systems. The early stage featured single, unconnected systems for separate business functions. In stages

3 and 4 managers are linking systems together and using them to make radical changes to previously
55 separate processes. In stage 5 they are using common information systems based on the Internet to move information between organisations, often having direct electronic links with their customers.

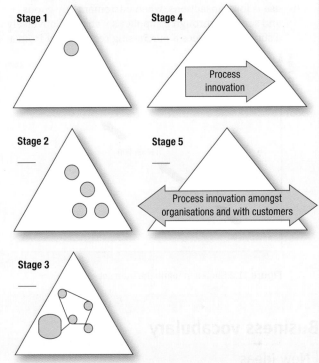

Figure 11.1 The widening effects of information systems

Managing over the Internet

D The significance of the Internet for everyone who
60 works in organisations cannot be overstated. It affects all aspects of organisational activity, enabling new forms of organisation and new ways of doing business (Cairncross, 2001). This includes selling a product or service over the Internet and using the Internet to
65 integrate all the required processes, from suppliers through to delivery to the customers. Another relevant term is an intranet, which is a private computer network operating within an organisation. It uses Internet standards and protocols and is protected
70 by various forms of security. Intranets operate as separate networks within the Internet. The opposite is an extranet, which is a closed collaborative network that uses the Internet to link businesses with specified suppliers, customers or other trading partners.
75 Extranets usually link to business intranets where information is accessible through a password system.

E The simplest Internet applications provide information, enabling customers to view products or other information on a company website; conversely

80 suppliers use their website to show customers what they can offer. Internet marketplaces are developing in which groups of suppliers in the same industry operate a collective website, making it easier for potential customers to compare terms through a single portal.

85 The next stage is to use the Internet for interaction. Customers enter information and questions about (for example) offers and prices. The system then uses the customer information, such as preferred dates and times of travel, to show availability and costs. A third

90 use is for transactions, when customers buy goods and services through a supplier's website. Conversely a supplier who sees a purchasing requirement from a business (perhaps expressed as a purchase order on a website) can agree electronically to meet the order.

95 The whole transaction, from accessing information through ordering, delivery and payment, can take place electronically. Finally, a company achieves integration when it links its own IS and then links them to customers and suppliers: it becomes an e-business.

100 Dell Computing is a familiar example amongst many others. As customers decide the configuration of their computer and place an order, this information moves to the systems that control Dell's internal processes and those of its suppliers. Figure 11.2 shows these stages.

F Other companies use the Internet to create and orchestrate active customer communities. Examples include Kraft, Intel, Apple and Harley-Davidson. These communities enable the companies to become close to their customers, and to learn how best to improve a

110 product or service much more quickly than is possible through conventional market research techniques. The Internet is evidently challenging many established ways of doing business. Combined with political changes, this is creating a wider, often global, market for many

115 goods and services. The challenge for managers is to make profitable use of these possibilities. This includes looking beyond technology – which receives most attention – to the wider organisation.

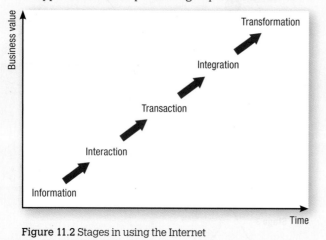

Figure 11.2 Stages in using the Internet

Source: D Boddy, *Management, an introduction*, Pearson, Harlow 2007, pp.383–387

Business vocabulary

New ideas

The following words are all connected to different stages of innovation. Use them to describe how new ideas start and develop, through to when they are used by many people.

1 Look back at the text on page 45. Find words in paragraph B ('Major developments') for definitions a–d.

a accepted, or started to use something new (v)
a _ _ _ t _ _

b the introduction of a new idea or product (n)
l _ _ _ c _

c an important discovery or event that helps to solve a problem or situation (n)
b _ _ _ _ th _ _ _ gh

d something new which has never been made before (n)
i _ _ _ _ _ i _ n

2 The words in *italics* in sentences 1–4 can be used as synonyms of words in 1. Match them to a–d in 1.

1 People were quick to *embrace* the new idea. ___

2 The development of wireless technology was an important *innovation* in the world of communication. ___

3 There was much interest in the company after the *unveiling* of its new product range. ___

4 Micro- and nano-technology were vital *advances* in the development of mobile technology. ___

3 Complete sentences a–d with two possible words from 1 and 2.

a Many people are still waiting for a number of key scientific _____ / _____ in key medical areas such as AIDS and cancer.

b Younger generations are often quicker to _____ / _____ technological developments than older generations.

c When Apple announces the _____ / _____ of a new product there is usually much media interest.

d The _____ / _____ of the micro-chip changed modern society significantly.

4 Write three sentences using vocabulary from 1 and 2 to describe innovations that you feel have been the most important in the last 100 years.

Writing skills

A | SKILLS REVIEW Synthesizing

To 'synthesize' means to incorporate information from other people's ideas into your work in an acceptable way, using techniques such as paragraphing, paraphrasing and summarizing and referencing. If you can synthesize effectively, your writing will be more authoritative.

1 Put typical paragraph features a–d into a logical order.

  a a short explanation to support the main idea
  b a concluding sentence
  c the identification of a weakness or problem
  d a topic sentence giving the main idea of the paragraph

2 A quote can come at any stage of a paragraph, but often comes at one particular point.

  a At which stage in 1 do you think it is quite common to include a quote?
  b What would the role of the other sentences be in relation to the quote?

3 A range of verbs can be used to introduce a quote. Do the verbs in the list usually argue for (F), usually argue against (A) or are they neutral (N)?

  to acknowledge ____   to describe ____
  to assert ____   to dispute ____
  to caution ____   to maintain ____
  to contend ____   to state ____
  to define ____

4 Agree in pairs.

  a What is the difference between a direct and an indirect quote?
  b What information do you need to include in a text when you use information from another source? Is it the same in both direct and indirect quotations?

5 Read essay extracts a and b that have used source text from the text on page 45 (lines 45–47).

  a Correct the direct quote.

  > According to David Boddy (p.383), linking mobile phones to the Internet has led to the explosive growth of the 'Wireless Internet'.

  b Correct the indirect quote.

  > David (2007) states that 'Connecting mobile devices to the Internet has resulted in significant growth in the Wireless Internet.'

6 Quoting indirectly involves either paraphrasing or summarizing. Which features a–d relate to paraphrasing (P) and which to summarizing (S)?

  a focuses on the main ideas   ____
  b often involves the topic sentence   ____
  c focuses on the main ideas of individual sentences   ____
  d often keeps the same length as the original   ____

7 Read the sentence from the text, then read the paraphrase.

  > Linking mobile phones to the Internet has led to the explosive growth of the 'Wireless Internet', which in effect liberates the computer from the desktop, enabling information to pass readily between people wherever they are. (lines 45–49)

  The explosion in wireless technology has largely been caused by connecting mobile phones to the Internet, so as a result, people are able to send data from any location.

  Tick the key changes in the paraphrase.

  grammar ____   meaning ____   punctuation ____
  spelling ____   vocabulary ____ word order ____

B | Writing practice

1 Write a paraphrase of this sentence from the text on page 46. You could use some of the words suggested in the list.

  allow   make better   slow   traditional   understand

  > These communities enable the companies to become close to their customers, and to learn how best to improve a product or service much more quickly than is possible through conventional market research techniques. (lines 107–111)

2 Read the highlighted extract in paragraph F in the text on page 46. Then write a paragraph of your own, synthesizing the information appropriately. Paraphrase or summarize, and include direct or indirect quotation using the source details.

Research task

Research an important innovation. How has it impacted on society? Synthesize the information you find into one or two paragraphs.

Study focus

Look at five changes that may happen during someone's career. Rank them from 1 (most) to 5 (least) difficult for you. Explain your ranking.

- getting promoted   ___
- your company being merged with another   ___
- changing companies   ___
- getting a new boss   ___
- retiring   ___

Reading strategies

A | Reading quickly for specific information

1 Scan sections B and C in the extract from an academic textbook. Which headings are paragraphs a–f related to, 'Current problems' or 'OD activities'?

   a Mergers/acquisitions

   b Team-building activities

   c Survey-feedback activities

   d Organizational decline/revitalization

   e Conflict management

   f Large group interventions

2 Which sections a–f in 1 are 1–6 linked to?

   1 enhance cohesiveness   ___

   2 questionnaires   ___

   3 disappointing financial results   ___

   4 lack of innovation and high turnover   ___

   5 arguments   ___

   6 fundamental organizational change   ___

B | Reading closely for detailed information

1 Read paragraph A in detail. What is the main aim of Organization Development?

2 In pairs, Student A read 'OD activities', Student B read 'Current problems'.

   Student A, ask B …

   a Why do mergers and acquisitions fail financially?

   b How can Organization Development techniques help in a situation of decline or revitalization?

   c What are some of the reasons behind conflict in today's organizations?

   d Why should companies not focus on specific problems?

   Student B, ask A …

   e How can Organization Development help cross-departmental teams?

   f What happens after the employees have completed their surveys?

   g Who is involved in large group intervention?

   h What are the benefits of involving such a large group of people in the change?

C | Identifying the writer's point of view

1 Which of the following, a–c, do you think describes the writer's opinion of Organization Development?

   a positive about its impact

   b neutral

   c negative about its impact

2 Read section C ('OD activities') again.

   a Which technique do you think the author feels is the most effective of the OD activities described?

   b <u>Underline</u> the parts that make you think this.

   c Compare your answers to **2a** and **b** in pairs. Explain your reasons for underlining.

D | Reacting to the text

1 Read section B ('Current problems') again. Put the three problems into order from 1 (hardest) to 3 (easiest) to deal with, in your opinion. Discuss in pairs.

   ___ Mergers/acquisitions

   ___ Organizational decline/revitalization

   ___ Conflict

2 Are the problems the responsibility of the individual or the organization? Mark the line to show your opinion. Discuss in pairs.

Mergers/acquisitions

Decline/revitalization

Conflict

Organization development

A Organization development (OD) is a planned, systematic process of change that uses behavioral science knowledge and techniques to improve an organization's health and effectiveness through its ability to adapt to
5 the environment, improve internal relationships, and increase learning and problem-solving capabilities. OD focuses on the human and social aspects of the organization and works to change attitudes and relationships among employees, helping to strengthen
10 the organization's capacity for adaptation and renewal.

Current problems

B OD can help managers address at least three types of current problems.

   1. **Mergers/acquisitions.** The disappointing financial results of many mergers and acquisitions are caused
15 by the failure of executives to determine whether the administrative style and corporate culture of the two companies fit. Executives may concentrate on potential synergies in technology, products, marketing, and control systems but fail to recognize that two firms
20 may have widely different values, beliefs, and practices. These differences create stress and anxiety for employees, and these negative emotions affect future performance. Cultural differences should be evaluated during the acquisition process, and OD experts can be
25 used to smooth the integration of two firms.

   2. **Organizational decline/revitalization.** Organizations undergoing a period of decline and revitalization experience a variety of problems, including a low level of trust, lack of innovation,
30 high turnover, and high levels of conflict and stress. The period of transition requires opposite behaviors, including confronting stress, creating open communication, and fostering creative innovation to emerge with high levels of productivity. OD techniques
35 can contribute greatly to cultural revitalization by managing conflicts, fostering commitment, and facilitating communication.

   3. **Conflict management.** Conflict can occur at any time and place within a healthy organization.
40 For example, a product team for the introduction of a new software package was formed at a computer company. Made up of strong-willed individuals, the team made little progress because members could not agree on project goals. At a manufacturing firm,
45 salespeople promised delivery dates to customers that were in conflict with shop supervisor priorities for assembling customer orders. In a publishing company, two managers disliked each other intensely. They argued at meetings, lobbied politically against each
50 other, and hurt the achievement of both departments. Organization Development efforts can help resolve these kinds of conflicts, as well as conflicts that are related to growing diversity and the global nature of today's organizations.

55 However, to be truly valuable to companies and employees, Organization Development practitioners go beyond looking at ways to settle specific problems. Instead, they become involved in broader issues that contribute to improving organizational life, such as
60 encouraging a sense of community, pushing for an organizational climate of openness and trust, and making sure the company provides employees with opportunities for personal growth.

OD Activities

C OD consultants use a variety of specialized techniques
65 to help meet OD goals. Three of the most popular and effective are the following:

   1. **Team-building activities.** Team building enhances the cohesiveness and success of organizational groups and teams. For example, a series of OD exercises can
70 be used with members of cross-departmental teams to help them learn to act and function as a team. An OD expert can work with team members to increase their communication skills, facilitate their ability to confront one another, and help them accept common goals.

75 2. **Survey-feedback activities.** Survey feedback begins with a questionnaire distributed to employees on values, climate, participation, leadership, and group cohesion within their organization. After the survey is completed, an OD consultant meets with groups of
80 employees to provide feedback about their responses and the problems identified. Employees are engaged in problem solving based on the data.

   3. **Large group interventions.** In recent years, the need for bringing about fundamental organizational
85 change in today's complex, fast-changing world prompted a growing interest in the applications of OD techniques to large group settings. The large-group intervention approach brings together participants from all parts of the organization – often including
90 key stakeholders from outside the organization as well – to discuss problems or opportunities and plan for change. A large group intervention might involve 50 to 500 people and last several days. The idea is to include everyone who has a stake in change, gather
95 perspectives from all parts of the system, and enable people to create a collective future through sustained, guided dialogue.

Large-group interventions reflect a significant shift in the approach to organizational change from earlier OD
100 concepts and approaches. In the newer approach, the focus is on the entire system, which takes into account the organization's interaction with its environment. The source of information for discussion is expanded

105 to include customers, suppliers, community members, even competitors, and this information is shared widely so that everyone has the same picture of the organization and its environment. The acceleration of change when the entire system is involved can be remarkable. In addition, learning occurs across all

110 parts of the organization simultaneously, rather than in individuals, small groups, or business units. The result is that the large-group approach offers greater possibilities for fundamental, radical transformation of the entire culture, whereas the traditional approach

115 creates incremental change in a few individuals or small groups at a time.

Source: R Daft, *New era of management*, Mason, Ohio 2008, pp.287–290

Glossary

synergies (line 18): (n) combined power of things working together

fostering (line 33): (v) encouraging the development of something

fundamental (line 84): (adj) basic

sustained (line 96): (adj) continuing

radical (line 113): (adj) from the root

Business vocabulary

A | Ownership of a company

The following words are all associated with changes in ownership of a company.

1 Which word in italics do definitions a–d describe?

 a the joining together of two companies

   1 After the *merger* of company A and company B, it took some time to work out which company had strengths in which areas.

   2 The *acquisition* of the firm resulted in little change in day-to-day work, just a new owner.

 b making savings in staffing or costs

   1 The *integration* of the two departments meant that a whole new IT system had to be created.

   2 Reducing the number of branches meant that a number of *synergies* could be achieved.

 c the purchase of a company, usually by staff currently working for it

   1 The management *buyout* meant that whilst we had new owners, the people running the company remained the same.

   2 The company did not want to sell, but as the buyers' share increased to 51%, they were able to force a *takeover* of the company.

 d a person with an interest in a company

   1 Customers may not own the company but they are certainly a key *stakeholder* as without customers companies cannot exist.

   2 The *joint venture* meant that each company was independent but benefited from working together.

2 Write definitions for the four words not defined in 1.

B | Change verbs

The following verbs describe ideas of 'change' and how to deal with it.

1 Match to definitions 1–8 to verbs of change a–h.

 a enhance ___   e engage (in) ___
 b revitalize ___   f participate (in) ___
 c facilitate ___   g enable ___
 d accept ___   h resist ___

 1 to give new life or energy to something
 2 to fight against something or not accept it
 3 to make something easier
 4 to improve something
 5 to take part in something
 6 to agree with something or say yes to it
 7 to interest somebody in something
 8 to give somebody the ability to do something

2 Rewrite sentences a–h using a correct form of the word in bold.

 a After the talk, I felt completely ready to start again. **revitalize**

 b The training gave me the ability to deal with the situation effectively. **enable**

 c The company felt that people would enjoy being asked to take part in the project. **participate**

 d Many employees did not feel that the merger improved the company. **enhance**

 e Our manager was very experienced at making change easier. **facilitate**

 f They refused to agree with the terms of the merger. **accept**

 g The company tried to encourage the public to be interested in the discussion. **engage**

 h The employees refused to agree with the changes and went on strike. **resist**

Writing skills

A | Organizing ideas

Essays often require you to express an opinion. It is usually important to do two things with an opinion. Firstly, an opinion should be supported with a quote, fact or explanation. Secondly, an opinion should be expressed with some caution, to acknowledge that you realize the opinion is not a fact.

1 Put sentences a–d into the most logical order to make a paragraph.

a	However, many companies fail to make the improvements or savings they wish for.	___
b	As a result, companies that have mergered often perform financially worse than expected.	___
c	Companies often merger expecting to make savings in resources, staffing and technology.	___
d	One main reason for this is the fact that companies do not take into consideration corporate culture or administrative style (Daft, 2007).	___

2 Match the paragraph terms to sentences a–d in 1.

a statement ___

a counter opinion ___

a supporting quote, fact or explanation ___

a concluding sentence ___

B | Writing an argument

1 Look at statements a–f. Which ones do you think are a fact (F) and which are an opinion (O)?

a 500 takeovers occurred in 2008. ___

b Many mergers do not achieve the results expected. ___

c Acquisitions were common in 2009. ___

d Conflict does not only occur in weak companies. ___

e To influence change in a whole company it needs to be dealt with at a level beyond the individual. ___

f The merger resulted in 200 job cuts. ___

2 Put the expressions into arguments 'for' or 'against'.

as well as	furthermore	having said that
however	in addition	moreover
nevertheless	on the other hand	

For	Against

3 In pairs, choose one statement each from a–f in 1.

a Respond to it with either an agreeing opinion using a 'for' expression, or a counter opinion using an 'against' expression from the list in 2.

b Find a quote, fact or explanation from the text on page 49, or from your own knowledge, to develop your opinion.

Many mergers do not achieve the results expected. However, some mergers can be successful. One example of this is …

c Tell a partner your opinion.

4 What is the difference between sentences a and b?

a Large group intervention is the most effective OD tool.

b Large group intervention is perhaps the most effective OD tool.

5 Look at the expressions in the list to add caution. In pairs, think of more expressions.

could be argued that   might   perhaps   suggests

6 Use the expressions in 5 to make sentences a–d more cautious.

a Mergers have a negative impact on company morale.

b Team-building improves cohesiveness.

c Conflict occurs in every company.

d OD techniques contribute to cultural revitalization.

C | Writing practice

1 Make opinions a–c more cautious. Then write a response to the statement.

a Marketing campaigns are the main reason a company is successful.

b Conflict is largely the result of poor management.

c Poor communication skills create difficult working relationships.

2 Think about your opinion on the following statement.

Effective change involves large groups not individuals.

Write a paragraph EITHER in favour of OR against the statement. Include …

- a supported opinion (using the text or your own reading).
- cautious language.

Research task

Research a merger or acquisition. What challenges did it face, and how did it overcome these? Write a paragraph EITHER in favour of OR against it.

13 Understanding the market

Study focus

1 Think of a product or service that you have bought in the last year. What influenced you the most when you bought it? Rate each factor out of 5.

	little influence ——→ big influence				
Price	1	2	3	4	5
Brand	1	2	3	4	5
Quality	1	2	3	4	5
Advertising	1	2	3	4	5

2 Is there anything else that influences you?

3 Which factors in 1 do you think are most important for a small company when trying to influence customers to buy?

Reading strategies

A | Understanding main and supporting ideas

1 Quickly read the extract from an academic textbook. Match main ideas 1–3 to section headings B–D.

1 A wide range of people, such as suppliers, governments and employees, can influence the success of a company. ____

2 An approach which starts from a wide view of the whole market and becomes more specific. ____

3 An approach which starts with a small base of customers and expands from there. ____

B Top-down theory
C Bottom-up practices
D Identifying targets other than new customers

2 Which of the main ideas 1–3 in 1 do statements a–f support?

a Companies need to divide the market and target different sections of the market.

b Developing relations is important to the success of small businesses.

c The company understands the needs of its small group of customers very well.

d Products need to be differentiated from those of competitors.

e Employees need to believe in the aims of the company.

f New customers are needed to help grow a business by word-of-mouth recommendation.

B | Reading closely for detailed information

1 Student A, read section B, 'Top-down theory'.

a How are customers profiled?

b What two criteria do companies use to decide on their target consumer?

c What is the main aim of the market position?

Student B, read section C, 'Bottom-up practices'.

d How is bottom-up different from top-down?

e How much contact does a small business tend to have with its customers?

f Is small business expansion always planned?

2 Summarize your findings to your partner. What are the main differences between the strategies of small and big businesses?

C | Finding support for an opinion

Read section D. Match reasons for success a–f to types of markets 1–6 in the text.

a 'Our product is quite similar to others on the market, but we highlighted the differences well, so it was easy to sell.' ____

b 'We had links with people who liked our services, and word-of-mouth recommendations really increased our sales.' ____

c 'A whole range of people have an effect on the success of our company.' ____

d 'Our staff are the main reason for our success. We are always careful about who we hire.' ____

e 'Most of our contracts come from local governments, so it's important we maintain good relationships with them.' ____

f 'It's more important to keep our existing customers happy than to focus on finding new ones.' ____

D | Reacting to the text

Discuss in pairs.

• Think about a magazine, website, newspaper or TV channel. What is the profile of the people who purchase / watch these? How could companies target this segment?

• Look at the six markets in section D of the text. Rank them in order from 1 (most important) to 6 (least important) for a small business.

Marketing strategy: top-down or bottom-up?

A Research has confirmed that entrepreneurs that successfully grow their businesses ^a define their target markets more clearly than those running non-growth firms. A common weakness of small firms is their over-
5 reliance on small numbers of customers. However, a related strength is that owner-managers often identify closely with specific customers whose needs are well known to them.

Top-down theory

B Marketing textbooks recommend a process that
10 takes a market overview as the starting point and narrows this down to specific target markets through the three stages of ^b segmentation, ^c targeting and ^d positioning. This represents a 'top-down' approach:

- **Segmentation**: The division of the market into
15 groups of buyers with different needs is achieved through research that ^e profiles customers. The profiling uses demographic, psychological and other buyer-behaviours.
- **Targeting**: ^f Evaluation of the attractiveness of each
20 segment and selection of the target segment are based on the issues of market attractiveness and the company's ability to compete.
- **Positioning**: Finally, a market position is selected and communicated which ^g differentiates the product/
25 service from competitors. The company needs to offer something different from competitor products or services.

This process implies that an organization is able to take an objective overview of the markets it serves before
30 selecting ones to concentrate on.

Bottom-up practices

C Although successful entrepreneurs do seem good at carefully targeting certain customers, the processes they use to achieve this do not seem to match the three stages described above. Evidence suggests that
35 successful smaller businesses practise a 'bottom-up' targeting process. The organization begins by serving the needs of a few customers and then expands gradually as experience and resources allow. The stages of entrepreneurial targeting are:
40 - ^h Identification of market opportunity. An opportunity is recognized by matching innovative ideas to the resources of a small enterprise. The opportunity is tested through trial and error in the marketplace, based on the entrepreneur's intuitive
45 expectations. Sometimes, but not often, these are supported by more formal research.
- **Attraction of an initial customer base.** Certain customers are attracted to the service or product. However, as the entrepreneur is in regular contact
50 with these customers, he or she gets to know their preferences and needs.

- **Expansion through more of the same.** The entrepreneur expands the initial customer base by looking for more customers of the same profile. In
55 many cases, this is not a deliberate process. It is left to the initial customers who recommend the business to others with similar needs to their own. A target customer group emerges and grows, but not in a structured and planned way.
60 A bottom-up targeting process has advantages over the top-down approach. It requires fewer resources and is more flexible and adaptable to implement – attributes which play to small business strengths. However, it is less certain of success and can take longer to enter the
65 market to full potential – issues that characterize many small firms.

Identifying targets other than new customers

D Target markets are not only concerned with customers in the normal sense of the term. Other groups of people, from suppliers to local planners, can directly
70 and indirectly influence the fortunes of small firms.
Small businesses survive in their changeable environment not only by successfully marketing to those who buy their products or services, but also by developing important relationships with
75 other individuals and organizations. Suppliers, bank managers, investors, advisors, trade associations, local government and public authorities may be as vital as customers to a small business's success. Marketing can target any organization or individual that can
80 have a positive or negative effect on the small firm. Relationship marketing theorists have attempted to identify these other markets more specifically in the six market model:

1 **Internal markets** are made up of individuals
85 within an organization whose behaviour and attitudes affect the performance of the business. Selling the aims and strategies of a small business to employees, shareholders and family members helps everyone concerned work towards common goals.
90 2 **Recruitment markets** are made up of potential employees. The aim of marketing here is to attract a sufficient number of well-motivated and trained employees. Particularly in small service businesses, employees have become a key marketing influence.
95 3 **Supplier markets** can be important to a small business's ability to service its customers. Suppliers are often vital in providing goods and services on time and at the right price. They can also be influential in passing on recommendations to potential customers.
100 4 **Influence markets** are made up of organizations and individuals that can influence the marketing environment. There are many such potential 'influencers' on small businesses, from local government planners to trade associations.

105 **5 Referral markets** are sources of word-of-mouth recommendations, other than customers. Small firms may be recommended by other local businesses, professional advisors (lawyers, accountants and consultants), and people who may not be direct
110 customers of the business.
6 Customer markets shift the emphasis from customer acquisition to customer retention through the development of mutually beneficial, long-term relationships. The aim of this type of marketing is to
115 turn new customers into regularly purchasing clients, who become strong supporters of the business and an active source of referrals. They help find new customers and may also contribute to the development of new business opportunities.

120 This seems to match the realities of entrepreneurial marketing which relies on identifying important customer groups and developing meaningful and long-term relationships with them.

Source: D Stokes & N Wilson, *Small business management and entrepreneurship*, Thomson Learning 2006, pp.363–367

Glossary

narrow down (line 11): (v) focus gradually on a smaller area
trial and error (line 43): (expression) trying, making mistakes and trying again in order to find the best way
emerges (line 58): (v) becomes visible
mutually (line 113): (adv) affecting both of two groups in the same way

Business vocabulary

A | Marketing

The following expressions are all associated with 'marketing' theories and activities.

1 **Look at the verbs in bold in sentences a–h. Find the verbs, or other forms of the word, in blue in the text on page 53. Use the context to write definitions of each verb.**

a It is important for companies **to define** who their customer is. (see line 2)

to define means 'to describe in detail'

b Once a market has been defined it is important **to segment** customers into groups. (see line 12)

c Marketing is often designed **to target** a specific group. (see line 12)

d A company needs **to position** itself or its products so that it is different from its competitors. (see line 13)

e The company decided **to profile** its consumers by looking at their spending habits and social class. (see line 16)

f They decided **to evaluate** the strengths and weaknesses of competitor's products. (see line 19)

g The company tried **to differentiate** itself from competitors by offering after-sales services. (see line 24)

h One of the main aims was **to identify** opportunities to expand the business in the future. (see line 40)

2 **Use verbs from 1 to complete the text.**

Many small businesses start because an individual has been able to ¹_____ a market opportunity. As a result, many small companies do not follow the traditional pattern of having to ²_____ their

market into groups, to ³_____ their customers with specific marketing, or to ⁴_____ themselves differently against competitors. Also, because they know their customers very well, they do not need to ⁵_____ their customers nor ⁶_____ exactly what the customer wants. However, to expand the company it may be necessary to ⁷_____ the company's strengths and weaknesses in comparison to competitors, so that they are able to ⁸_____ any new ideas from other products in the marketplace.

B | Collocations with 'market'

1 **Place the words in the list either before or after *market* to make common collocations.**

customer	opportunity	overview	place
position	recruitment	referral	target

2 **Check your answers against the highlighted words in the text on page 53.**

3 **Explain to a partner how a–c are important for a small business.**

a the referral market
b the market position
c the recruitment market

Writing skills

A | Showing cause and effect

A lot of academic writing is based on a 'cause and effect' relationship. This means looking at an event, situation or idea, and analysing what was the reason (= cause) and what is the result (= effect). Sometimes the cause is identified first, and sometimes the effect is identified first.

1 Look at sentences a–e. <u>Underline</u> the 'cause', and circle the 'effect'.

> (Sales have increased) because of <u>the marketing campaign</u>.

   a The outcome of the recruitment strategy was a much higher qualified group of staff.
   b Word-of-mouth marketing often leads to increased sales.
   c Customer loyalty has increased; consequently the business is more stable.
   d When a small company knows its customers well it is able to target their needs effectively.
   e Small businesses survive on account of successful marketing.

2 Use four of the expressions in the list to complete sentences a–d.

   accordingly   consequence   consequently   for this reason
   hence   owing to   since   so

   a _____ so many small companies start up every year, it is inevitable that many go bankrupt.
   b The _____ of poor sales can often be bankruptcy.
   c Bankruptcies are higher in smaller companies _____ the lack of differentiation in products and services.
   d Many owners of small businesses do not have a clear business plan, _____ they frequently go out of business.

3 Practise making 'cause and effect' sentences. Use expressions from 2 to join ideas a–d to ideas 1–4. Use correct punctuation.

   a top companies often have large marketing budgets
   b small companies have small marketing budgets
   c small businesses often rely on trade from larger companies, and
   d many contracts come from governments, and

   1 often suffer from cash flow problems due to slow payments
   2 they rely on word-of-mouth recommendation
   3 they often follow a top-down marketing strategy
   4 it is important for them to maintain good relationships with these groups

4 Complete sentences a–d with words/phrases from the list.

   impact on   origin of   outcome to   precedents for

   a Market knowledge can have a positive _____ customer retention.
   b There are a number of _____ using such a strategy.
   c Managers clearly hope to achieve a positive _____ all decisions.
   d The _____ many small businesses is the desire to meet a particular consumer need.

B | Writing practice

1 Look at the 'key situation' and the examples of causes and effects. In pairs, add more causes and effects.

'BANKRUPTCY'

Causes	Effects
poor marketing	*unemployment*
lack of capital	*wasted stock*
_____	_____
_____	_____
_____	_____

2 Write one or two paragraphs describing the main causes and effects of bankruptcy. Use linkers and correct punctuation.

Research task

Choose a company that has a number of different brands, such as a car company. Think about its possible top-down strategy.

- How have they segmented their market?
- How do they target the different segments?
- How have they positioned their brands against other companies?

Think of some reasons why they might have done this.

Study focus

1 Different cultures associate feelings with different colours. What do these colours represent to you?

black   **blue**   green   orange

red   white   yellow

2 Match a colour in 1 to countries/things a–g.

a good luck in China _____

b envy in Germany _____

c money in the USA _____

d love in Japan _____

e death in India _____

f patriotism in New Zealand _____

g very positive in Nigeria, Yoruba _____

3 How might colour associations be important in business?

Reading strategies

A | Predicting content using signposting

1 Read the main heading and the introduction (para. A) of an extract from an academic textbook. Which two of a–d do you think will be included in the text?

a which products to sell in which markets

b how to change a product for a market

c which marketing strategies work best in different countries

d problems translating promotional messages

2 Read the text and check your answers.

3 Carefully read the rest of the text. Match topic sentences 1–7 to paragraphs B–H.

1 ___

> When communicating with consumers in different parts of the world, the promotional message must be consistent with the language and customs of the particular target society.

2 ___

> International marketers frequently neglect to modify their products to meet local customs and tastes.

3 ___

> Consider some other examples.
> * A soft-drink company attempted to translate its popular Western slogan into Chinese.

4 ___

> Color is also a critical variable in international marketing, because the same color often has different meanings in different cultures.

5 ___

> Kellogg's, the giant cereal company, has attempted to avoid the numerous 'cultural traps' that are associated with cross-cultural marketing of food in its international expansion.

6 ___

> Product names and promotional phrases can also cause considerable problems for international marketers.

7 ___

> Still another example showed that when Oreos were introduced to Japan, Nabisco reduced the amount of sugar in the cookie (the box promoted them as having a 'bitter twist') to meet Japanese tastes.

B | Identifying the writer's point of view

Tick any of 1–5 that match the writer's opinions.

1 Many companies do not understand how to operate in different markets. ___

2 Cultures do not change over time so markets remain the same. ___

3 What a product looks like does not matter as long as it is marketed well. ___

4 Companies are getting better at operating internationally. ___

5 The whole name, image and product might need to change to fit a market. ___

Glossary

deaf (line 26): (adj) not able to hear

ceiling (line 43): (n) the inside surface of a room when you look above you

corpse (line 80): (n) dead body

grave (line 90): (n) place where someone is buried when they die

Marketing mistakes: a failure to understand differences

A In most cases, the risk for marketers in international marketing is not knowing whether the product, the promotional appeal, the pricing policy, or the retail channels that are effective in one country will work in
5 other countries. Furthermore, there are difficulties in trying to determine what specific changes should be made to ensure acceptance in each foreign market. The following examples of some international marketing errors illustrate that failure to adapt marketing strategy
10 to the target market's distinctive cultural features can lead to costly mistakes.

Product problems

B [...] American marketers who sell food products in Japan frequently learn the hard way (through poor sales performance) that they must alter traditional
15 product characteristics. For example, Snapple failed to sustain sales momentum in Japan because consumers preferred clearer, less sweet iced tea. It appears that Snapple was either unwilling or too slow to alter its ingredients to conform to local Japanese tastes.

C [...] It has learned to make careful distinctions between the Irish, who consume 17 pounds of cereal per person per year (the highest rate in the world), and the French, Italians, and Greeks, whose small breakfasts tend not to include cereal. Indeed, a recent
25 article discussing Kellogg's attempt to market cereals in Europe was titled 'Europe is deaf to Snap! Crackle! Pop!' The story did note that some European moms were purchasing cereal for their children, and that cultural changes on the Continent might make bigger
30 breakfasts essential.

D [...] However, some Japanese consumers still considered them too sweet and told the company that they 'just wanted to eat the base' without the cream. Nabisco introduced, very late, new Petit Oreo
35 Non-Cream cookies that consisted of single wafers without the cream. To avoid such problems, marketers must discover in advance whether the physical characteristics of their products will be acceptable to the new market. When IKEA opened its first store in
40 the Philadelphia area, it sold European-sized curtains that did not fit American windows. The founder of IKEA once remarked, jokingly, that 'Americans just won't lower their ceilings to fit our curtains'.

E [...] For example, consider the color blue. In Holland,
45 it stands for warmth; in Iran, it represents death; in Sweden, it means coldness; in India, it suggests purity. Furthermore, yellow, which represents warmth in the United States, means infidelity in France. Pepsodent made a mistake when it tried to sell its toothpaste in
50 Southeast Asia by promising white teeth. In that part of the world, chewing betel nuts is considered an elite habit and, consequently, brownish-red teeth are viewed

as a status symbol. Thus Pepsodent's slogan, 'You'll wonder where the yellow went', did not help to sell the
55 product. It is critical that the colors of products and packages convey the proper meaning in the countries in which they are marketed. For example, just before an American necktie manufacturer shipped its first order to Japan, their customer asked about the color of
60 the gift boxes. When told they are white, the Japanese customer requested red. In Japan, the color white is associated with death.

Promotional problems

F [...] International marketers have faced various problems in communicating with widely different
65 consumer groups. For example, the 7-Up Company's highly successful 'uncola' theme, developed for the U.S. market, was considered inappropriate for many foreign markets because it did not translate well into other languages. Similarly, learning from earlier mistakes,
70 multinational firms like P&G and Ford now work harder to be responsive to particular tastes and values of local markets. For instance, they recently withdrew their sponsorship of television programming in some countries when the sex and violence of the shows were
75 judged to be too strong.

G [...] The word *clock* in Chinese sounds like the word *death*. The Chevrolet Nova did not sell well in Latin America because in Spanish the words *no va* mean 'it doesn't run'. GM also blundered with its 'body by
80 Fisher' tag line, which in Flemish translates into 'corpse by Fisher'. The U.S. government made a miscalculation when it moved to drop the word *North* from North American Free Trade Agreement (or to move from NAFTA to AFTA) so as to make it more inclusive.
85 The trouble began when Brazil pointed out that in Portuguese 'AFTA' sounded like the words that mean 'an open mouth sore'.

H [...] The resulting translation informed consumers if they drank the soft drink, their ancestors would come
90 out of their graves.
* The Rolls Royce Silver Mist is called the Silver Shadow in Germany, because *mist* in German means manure.
* Japan's number-one cosmetic maker, Shiseido, is a
95 name that 'is unpronounceable for Americans and hard to remember'.
* A U.S. baby care company advertising in Hungary showed a young woman holding her baby. But to the people of Hungary, the mother was unwed, because her
100 wedding ring was on her left hand. Hungarians wear their wedding bands on their right hand.

Source: from Schiffman, Leon; Kanuk, Leslie *Consumer Behaviour, 9th Edition*, © 2007, pp.386–389. Reprinted by permission of Pearson Education, Inc. Upper Saddle River, NJ.

Unit 14 | Selling across cultures

Business vocabulary

A | Meaning and significance

The following expressions are all used to show or describe the meaning of something.

1 Match pairs of words a and b to the correct definitions 1 or 2.

a stand for ___ b mean ___
1 to represent a particular idea or ideas
2 to have a particular significance

a represent ___ b suggest ___
3 to communicate an idea without proof
4 to be a sign or symbol for something

a point out ___ b convey ___
5 to tell someone something because you believe they do not know it
6 to express a thought or idea so that others understand it

a signify ___ b associate ___
7 to connect something with something else
8 to be a sign of something

2 Complete sentences a–h with the correct form of a word from 1. Sometimes more than one answer is possible.

a People commonly _____ China with communism.
b The word *handy* _____ mobile phone in German.
c He always _____ other people's lack of knowledge.
d They tried to _____ their feelings on the subject but without much success.
e The colour white _____ peace in many countries of the world.
f The rise in price definitely _____ that the government's policy isn't working.
g He is used in many marketing campaigns because his image _____ 'fair play' to many people.
h What colours _____ is important in advertising.

3 What do different colours represent in your country? Describe at least five, using words from 1 and 2.

B | Mistakes and difficulties

These nouns and verbs all relate to making or dealing with mistakes.

1 Match words a–h to definitions 1–8.

a an error (n) ___
b a costly mistake (n) ___
c to learn the hard way (v) ___
d to fail (v) ___
e to face a problem (v) ___
f to blunder (v) ___
g to miscalculate (v) ___
h trouble (unc n) ___

1 something that goes wrong with serious or expensive results
2 to make a stupid or careless mistake
3 to judge a situation badly
4 a mistake
5 to know something from making a mistake
6 to not succeed
7 to be presented with a difficult situation
8 problems or difficulties

2 Complete sentences a–h with words/phrases from 1.

a They only realized their mistake afterwards, and had _____ .
b It was a small _____ , and so did not cause much concern.
c They _____ to spot the error in time.
d He was in _____ for the insensitive cultural decisions he made.
e They _____ the number of books they were likely to sell.
f They _____ so badly that it had a major impact on the company's reputation.
g If we don't focus on job satisfaction now we will _____ with recruitment in the future.
h The lack of market knowledge was such a _____ the company nearly went bankrupt.

3 Write the noun forms of three verbs from 1.

to fail _____
to blunder _____
to miscalculate _____

4 Think about three mistakes you made, or difficult situations you faced. Describe them using words/ phrases from 1–3. Compare in pairs.

Writing skills

Understanding and using feedback

Teacher feedback will focus on a variety of areas, depending on the task you have been given. However, three common areas that teachers focus on are …

- grammar and vocabulary.
- text organization.
- supporting ideas.

1 You receive the following comment from a teacher. In pairs, discuss what type of mistakes you are looking for.

'You have a number of problems with word formation in your essay.'

2 <u>Underline</u> and correct the word formation mistakes in sentences a–d.

a The company was well representation at the conference.

_____

b The suggest was rejected for being inadequate.

_____

c It was a cost error of judgement.

_____

d The company is association with quality products.

_____

3 You receive the following comment from a teacher on the paragraph below.

'Your paragraphing lacks a logical structure.'

Different colours have different connotations depending on the market. Companies also need to be careful when considering using the same brand name in different cultures. Colour plays a key role in the success of a product. Therefore companies may need to change the colour of a product depending on their significance in the target market. For example, in many cultures, the colour black represents death, yet in Iran, death is represented by the colour blue.

Read the paragraph. In pairs, discuss what might be wrong, and what type of mistakes you are looking for.

4 Rewrite the paragraph in 3 so that it is well-structured and clearly focused.

5 You receive the following comment from a teacher on the paragraph below.

'Your ideas lack cohesion.'

One of the main challenges faced by a company entering a new international market is not knowing this market well. On the other hand, companies need to know how to adapt their product to different markets. Furthermore, even a brand such as Coca-Cola is adapted to meet different market needs such as the sweetness of the drink. Finally, a successful company is likely to be one that researches the market well before entering it.

Read the paragraph. In pairs, discuss what might be wrong, and what type of mistakes you are looking for.

6 <u>Underline</u> and correct any mistakes with the use of connectors in the paragraph in 5.

7 You receive the following comment from a teacher on the paragraph below.

'Your opinions are at times quite subjective.'

Companies need to understand their target market well. A product that is successful in one market will not necessarily be successful in another market. There may be characteristics of a product that do not appeal, even in markets that businesses may perceive to be culturally similar. If these factors are not considered prior to entering a market, this can prove to be a costly mistake.

Read the paragraph. In pairs, discuss what type of mistakes you are looking for, and how you could improve it.

8 Find support from the text on page 57 to strengthen the argument in the paragraph in 7. Rewrite the paragraph.

Research task

Look through the writing sections of this book again. Begin to develop a checklist that you can use to edit your own work in future, e.g.

Is there a clear topic sentence?

Does everything relate to the main idea?

Study focus

1 From 1–10, how do you rate your personal likelihood of being stressed?

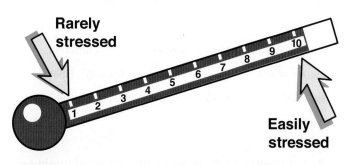

Rarely stressed

Easily stressed

2 Compare your ratings in pairs. Explain …

   a what makes you stressed.
   b what stops you from being stressed.

Reading strategies

A | Predicting content using background knowledge

1 In pairs, think of three examples for each category.

   • Causes of work-related stress
   • Effects on job performance
   • How to control stress

2 You are going to read a newspaper article on work-related stress. Choose one option for paragraphs A–G to predict what the article will say.

   A Every year stress-related illnesses cost the UK
   1 £13 million.
   2 over £3 billion.

   B Stress affects job performance by
   1 making people tired.
   2 making people give up.

   C Work-related stress is caused by
   1 poor job security.
   2 too much to do.

   D Work-related stress can be controlled by
   1 more policies.
   2 giving control to employees.

   E Giving autonomy to employees
   1 creates inefficiency.
   2 increases efficiency.

   F Most companies
   1 control employees.
   2 allow employees to control their work.

   G Most companies give control to
   1 customers.
   2 managers.

3 Read the text and check your predictions.

B | Reading closely for detailed information

Read the text again and answer the questions.

1 How are stress and absence connected?
2 According to CIPD, is stress at work increasing or decreasing?
3 How does the government suggest dealing with the problem?
4 What are some of the main causes of stress, according to CIPD?
5 What are some of the main causes of stress, according to the HSE?
6 What determines whether a job is 'good'?
7 Who should make the decisions?
8 Do managers tighten or loosen control when there is a problem?
9 How can managers engage employees more in the organization?

C | Identifying arguments for and against

In the text, when does the writer argue 'for' and when does he argue 'against'? For statements 1–7, write for (F) or against (A). <u>Underline</u> the part of the text which tells you this.

1 Stress-minimizing techniques are a good method for controlling stress at work. (para. **B**) ____
2 Policies will not help to manage stress. (para. **D**) ____
3 A lack of control and confusion about roles leads to stress. (para. **D**) ____
4 Hard work and change can be positive. (para. **D**) ____
5 Decisions need to be made by senior management not the individual worker. (para. **E**) ____
6 Mobile phones have had a positive effect on freeing people up from desk-based work. (para. **F**) ____
7 The system needs to change. (para. **G**) ____

Get stress out of your system

A Like Victory in Europe and the Queen's birthday, stress is now considered to be so important that it has its own day. Stress at work is serious: it costs £3.7 billion and 13 million lost working days, according to estimates by
5 the Health and Safety Executive, with the unknowable costs thought to be much higher.

B 'Stress makes people stupid,' in the words of Daniel Goleman in Emotional Intelligence. It stops them thinking straight and doing their jobs properly. It
10 makes them give up psychologically before they start. It is also on the increase. In a recent survey by the Chartered Institute of Personnel and Development (CIPD), 40 per cent of employers reported a rise in stress-related absence. Innumerable individual
15 surveys find employees complaining of increasing stress as workloads and pressures intensify, leading to steadily declining job satisfaction, particularly in the public sector. Human Resources magazine talks of 'a silent epidemic'. The government is so concerned
20 that employers now have a legal obligation to have effective stress-minimising policies in place in the workplace. But hang on, there's a bit of a contradiction here. Where are these pressures coming from? From the organisations that are now being enjoined to install
25 stress-management schemes.

C Stress is the physical symptom in individuals of the darker side of organisational life. In a recent pamphlet, Demos talks of 'hyperorganisation': the relentless spiral of pressure from capital markets (and governments
30 apeing them) for ever more effort and efficiency – faster! longer! harder! Workloads, change, targets and management style all figure largely among stress generators, according to the CIPD. But even this is not enough. Increasingly, as Madeleine Bunting noted in
35 her book *Willing Slaves*, organisations demand not just physical effort, but employees are made to feel guilty if they don't give their souls too. No wonder people feel stressed.

D Like absence, to which it is closely related, stress
40 doesn't need managing with yet more policies, techniques, and check-boxes. It needs getting rid of, so it doesn't require managing at all. That might sound fanciful, but it's not. Consider the causes of stress, classified by the HSE as to do with (over-
45 demanding) workload, (lack of) autonomy, (poor) support, (low-trust) work relationships, (unclear) roles and (incomprehensible) change. But turn these around and they become stress neutralisers rather than creators. Research on what makes for a
50 'good' job invariably emphasises control over work as the number one determinant, followed by good relationships and support, a clearly understood role and security. As the Work Foundation points out, stress is psychological, pertaining to the individual. Where the

55 right psychological ingredients are in place individuals turn hard work and change into a positive challenge and opportunity for growth. And control over the job, clarity of roles and all the other elements of the good job aren't just stress-moderators for individuals: they
60 are essential components of good management in the 21st century, the only way organisations can move from today's outmoded mass-production management systems to the flexible, customer-centred organisations of tomorrow.

E Control, or autonomy, is critical. One of the most important qualities distinguishing 'lean' from traditional management systems is the placing of decision-making control with the people who do the work – enabling the assembly-line worker to stop the
70 line when there's a problem, or the call-centre agent to decide individually how to respond to a customer inquiry or complaint, for example. This is more efficient as well as more humane, or to put it another way it eliminates human as well as material waste.

F So why is lean management, despite some lip service, still so much the exception, rather than the rule? For the answer, we need to go back to control. Most Western companies are run from the top down. In this view, managers have to give orders (that's what hierarchy
80 is for), otherwise workers wouldn't know what to do. Given that initial premise, it's not surprising that most managers respond to any performance challenge by tightening control, not loosening it. A good example is the way mobile communication devices, touted as a
85 means of liberating people from office constraints, are in practice becoming the opposite: an additional means of surveillance which, in the words of one recent report, 'will simply translate into round-the-clock working for some employees'. Thus the remedy makes things
90 worse. No amount of well-meaning policies can prevent these tendencies from generating more stress.

G Turning organisations inside out so that orders come from customers, not remote senior managers and their computer schedules (more logical, no?) goes completely
95 against the grain for most managers, whose instinct is always to turn the pressure up and then try to mitigate its worst effects. But this just increases their own stress. Better to bite the bullet. Giving control back to people who perform the principal customer-related tasks
100 not only removes one of the principal causes of work-related stress for individuals but given proper support it can halt the vicious circle of hyperorganisation and set in train a benevolent one of engagement and improvement that benefits the entire organisation. In
105 other words, de-stress the system, not individuals: that way everyone benefits – including top managers, some of the (self-created) worst sufferers.

Source: S Caulkin, 'Get stress out of your system' in *The Observer*, www.guardian.co.uk 6 November 2005

Glossary

epidemic (line 19): (n) disease affecting many people at the same time

enjoined (line 24): (v) encouraged

relentless (line 28): (adj) constant

get rid of (line 41): (v) stop

humane (line 73): (adj) kind

lip service (line 75): (n) saying you agree with something but doing nothing about it

touted (line 84): (v) presented, sold persuasively

against the grain (line 95): (expression) something you would not normally do because it is unusual or wrong

bite the bullet (line 98): (expression) force yourself to do something unpleasant

Business vocabulary

A | Dealing with problems

The following expressions are all associated with 'problem-solving'.

1 Match two verbs to each heading.

| to address | to constrain | to eliminate | to liberate |
| to loosen | to mitigate | to tighten | to oversee |

More control

Less control

2 Match the other four verbs in 1 to definitions a–d.

a to get rid of completely _____

b to lessen the effect _____

c to give attention to _____

d to manage from a distance _____

3 Read about a manager dealing with a problem. Complete 1–6 with the correct form of verbs from 1.

I took a hands-off approach with my team, simply ¹_____ projects. I didn't believe in ²_____ them, as I felt it would hinder their creativity. I wanted to ³_____ them from the normal strict rules that many managers apply. However, I then found that I had to ⁴_____ my control of the team, as many did not perform to the standard I expected. I found that this ⁵_____ the problem to a certain extent, but it hasn't fully ⁶_____ the problems.

4 Answer questions a–d about the situation in 3. Use a form of the words in *italics*.

a Why did she *loosen* control of the team to start with?

b What problem did the manager have to *address*?

c Why did she have to *tighten* control of the team?

d Why do you think this change perhaps did not *eliminate* the problem?

B | Word formation: prefixes

A prefix is added to the start of a word to change the meaning of the word. A prefix can carry specific meaning, e.g. *over-demanding*: *over* = *too much*. A prefix can change the meaning to an opposite or negative form, e.g. *un*important = *not* important.

1 Complete words a–h with the prefixes in the list.

im x 1   in x 3   over x 2   un x 2

a ____numerable

b ____calculable

c ____estimate

d ____comprehensible

e ____whelming

f ____measurable

g ____manageable

h ____ruly

2 Rewrite sentences a–h, replacing the phrases in *italics* with words from 1. Remember to check the position of the adjective. Sometimes more than one answer is possible.

a His behaviour was *difficult to control*.

b My workload is *too much* for me.

c Government debts are at such a high level that they are *difficult to understand* for most people.

d There are *too many* options *to count*, which is making the decision very hard.

e The launch has been delayed by challenges *that are too difficult to work out*.

f They *guessed too high* the amount of money they would make.

g With poor leadership, employees can quickly become *very difficult to control*.

h The disastrous financial consequences of the bank's actions were *too big to measure*.

Writing skills

'Problem–solution' writing typically follows this pattern.

Stage 1 introduces and describes the problem.
Stage 2 suggests one or more solutions to the problem.
Stage 3 evaluates each solution.

The evaluation stage may come either immediately after each solution, or towards the end of the piece of writing.

A | Problem–solution–evaluation writing

1 Look at sentences a–f. Which are related to a problem (P), which to a solution (S) and which to an evaluation (E)?

a One in four people take time off work due to stress. ___

b Clearly defined roles might be one answer. ___

c Simply empowering people will not be enough unless workloads are also efficiently managed. ___

d Stress costs the UK economy billions of pounds per year. ___

e Empowering people may lead to a reduction in stress levels. ___

f Rules and regulations related to the management of stress are a common misguided approach to attempting to reduce stress. ___

2 Look back at the text on page 61. Write the paragraph letter in the table next to the type of function it has. If a paragraph has more than one function, write the letter in more than one place.

Problem	
Solution	
Evaluation	

3 Compare in pairs. Briefly define each Problem, Solution or Evaluation you identified in 2.

4 In pairs, read problems A–C. Write two possible solutions for each.

Problem A Sickness has increased at the company since workloads increased.

Problem B The turnover of staff has reached record levels.

Problem C Staff are becoming frustrated by decisions taken by managers who have little customer contact.

5 Look at the words in the list used in evaluative writing. Put them into the correct category.

comprehensive   efficient   flawed   fundamental
inadequate   misguided   notable   outmoded

Positive ➕	Negative ➖

6 Exchange your solutions to the problems in 4 with another pair. Write a brief evaluation of at least three of their solutions using at least one positive and one negative word from 5.

B | Writing practice

1 In pairs, brainstorm some different problems facing your country, e.g. political, social, economic, educational, other (what)?

2 Choose one problem and write at least three paragraphs.

- describe the problem
- describe a solution
- evaluate the solution

3 Exchange your writing with a partner.

a Have they provided enough details regarding the problem?

b How realistic is their solution?

c Is the solution specific enough or very generic in nature?

d Have they looked at both positives and negatives of the solution in their evaluation?

Research task

Find an article that describes a political, economic, social, business or other problem. Does the article offer any solutions? Does the article evaluate the solutions; if so, <u>underline</u> the evaluation language used.

Study focus

1 **Write down the following three numbers:**

the age you plan to retire _____

the oldest person you know still working _____

the best age to retire _____

2 **Compare your numbers in pairs. Discuss your reasons. How similar are you?**

3 **List three advantages and three disadvantages of having more old people in a company.**

Advantages	Disadvantages

Reading strategies

A | Reading quickly for general understanding

Read the newspaper article. Which statement, 1, 2 or 3, best completes a summary of the text?

The text describes …

1 the employment policy of a DIY store in the UK.
2 the ageing population of the UK.
3 the increase in and benefits of more people working until they are older.

B | Understanding main ideas

Tick the main idea, 1 or 2, for each paragraph A–H.

Paragraph A
1 the career of Sydney Prior ___
2 the increasing number of people over 60 working ___

Paragraph B
1 the similarities between England and the rest of Europe ___
2 the differences between England and the rest of Europe ___

Paragraph C
1 the likely decrease in the number of workers over 65 ___
2 the likely increase in the number of workers over 65 ___

Paragraph D
1 the benefits experienced by B&Q of having an older workforce ___
2 the difficulties faced by B&Q from having an older workforce ___

Paragraph E
1 the benefits experienced by two other companies of having an older workforce ___
2 the difficulties faced by two other companies from having an older workforce ___

Paragraph F
1 why companies want older people ___
2 why older people work ___

Paragraph G
1 the increasing job satisfaction in older workers ___
2 the decreasing job satisfaction in older workers ___

Paragraph H
1 more older people means more older workers ___
2 new laws mean more older workers are likely ___

C | Understanding supporting ideas

What supporting ideas are 1–8 related to?

1 11% (line 9)
2 rigid seniority system (line 26)
3 2 million (line 39)
4 a fifth (line 49)
5 customer service (line 62)
6 forced to work (line 73)
7 job security (line 87)
8 mixed-age workforce (line 101)

D | Reacting to the text

Which of the following do you agree/disagree with? Discuss your reasons in pairs.

• Older people should have to retire to allow younger people to develop their career.
• People should be able to work as long as they want.
• People work longer because they have to, not because they want to.
• Older people are better at customer service.
• Ageism is the same kind of discrimination as sexism or racism.

Second careers and the third age

A Sidney Prior was 77 when his second career as a customer adviser began at a B&Q garden centre in Wimbledon – he is still in the job 14 years later. 'Working with people of all ages gives youngsters the chance to learn a little from an old timer like myself,' he says, 'and they help to keep me young at heart.' The 91-year-old may not be typical, but he certainly represents a growing trend: more than 100,000 people aged over 60 found a new job in the year to November – a rise of 11%, the biggest ever, the Office for National Statistics (ONS) said yesterday. That means 1.1 million people over pensionable age are now working. Two-thirds are women.

B This rise is more surprising for coming at a time when overall unemployment and the number of jobless youngsters is going up. And it contrasts sharply with continental Europe, where far fewer older people are working. While about three-fifths of people aged 55 to 64 are still employed in Britain – well above the ratio in most other developed countries – only two out of five in Europe's biggest economy, Germany, are working. Peter Whiteford, of the Organisation for Economic Cooperation and Development (OECD), says: 'This is to a large part due to the UK's economic performance during the last years, which is much better than in a lot of other European countries.' But there are other reasons. Britain does not have a rigid seniority system as in France or Germany, where wages tend to rise with age. Higher labour costs for older workers cut demand. Also, the pension system in much of Europe still encourages people to retire early.

C The OECD, like the British government, predicts an increasing trend in hiring older people. 'The employment of people aged over 50 will continue to rise,' says Whiteford. This view is backed by the recent report of Lord Turner's pension commission, which assumes that most people will work well beyond the current state pension age as part of a national settlement to ensure decent incomes in later life. The ONS says Britain's workforce will expand by about 2 million people, to 32 million, over the next 15 years as people live longer and work longer. The number of workers aged 65 and over is expected to pick up by about 200,000 – a figure that may be conservative given the 100,000 rise in the past year alone.

D B&Q was the first British company to target older people. As the chain rapidly expanded in the late 1980s, it began to recruit people nobody else would hire: women returning after a career break and those over 50. Today more than a fifth of B&Q's 38,000 staff are over 50. Ian Cheshire, B&Q's chief executive, says: 'There are clear business benefits to employing a workforce that is age diverse and reflects the customer profile.' B&Q found that older workers were no less productive, despite preconceptions. Cheshire says: 'We have found that older workers have a great rapport with the customers, as well as a conscientious attitude and real enthusiasm for the job.'

E Sainsbury's, which has 170,000 staff, launched a campaign last June to recruit an extra 10,000 'mature' workers across Britain. Sainsbury's personnel manager, Jane Basley, says: 'People of that age bring a wealth of experience and maturity to their work, and their focus on customer service will undoubtedly have a positive effect on the shopping experience and help to drive sales.' Its rival Asda offers its 'Asda Goldies' flexible hours and benefits such as a week off unpaid on the birth of a grandchild. They found that their Goldies help to settle and train younger staff and are also appreciated by customers.

F But what drives older people to prefer working to relaxing at home or on a beach in Marbella? Is it only because pensions are too low to survive on? Paul Bates, of Help the Aged, says: 'It would not be true to say that all these people are forced to work because of poor pensions but that might be a reason for some. A lot of older people are working because they choose to do so – they want to remain in the world of work.'

G Older people have a lot to offer, such as reliability and experience, he says. Nevertheless, research also shows that employers do not manage and develop older workers effectively. Although they are more satisfied with their job than younger people, are healthy and do not have to work out of financial necessity, they exhibit the greatest fall in job satisfaction since the early 1990s. John Philpott, who carried out the study for the Chartered Institute of Personnel and Development, says: 'Although older workers have become more satisfied with their pay and have a stronger sense of job security, they are a lot less happy with the intrinsic quality of their jobs and the hours they work.'

H More companies are expected to hire older people once new laws on anti-age discrimination and retirement come into force in October. Changes to tax law in April mean workers will not have to retire before receiving their pension. This could be a big move towards flexible retirement, as employees aged 65 will be able to ask to keep on working, although the employer can refuse them. The new legislation is supported by business. In 1996, 18 of Britain's top companies set up the Employers Forum on Age (EFA), which now has more than 180 members that employ more than 3 million people. They promote the benefits of a mixed-age workforce but also admit that no members found it easy to introduce flexible retirement. 'There are many complications,' says Sam Mercer, director of EFA. 'We really must try to simplify things.'

Source: M Peters, 'Second careers and the third age' in *The Guardian*, www.guardian.co.uk 19 January 2006

Business vocabulary

A | Careers and employment

The following expressions all relate to careers or employment.

1 Read the example sentences and write definitions of bold words/phrases a–h.

a The **pensionable age** (n) in the UK is gradually increasing from 65 to 70 years old.

b The shop I work in pays me a weekly **wage** (n) of £75.

c I would like to **retire** (v) at 55 but I will probably have to work until I'm 65.

d Many shops **hire** (v) extra staff at Christmas.

e I found my job so stressful that I decided to take a **career break** (n) and travel for a year.

f Our company employs 20,000 members of **staff** (n) from a range of age groups.

g **Job security** (n) is not very good in my profession. I've lost my job ten times.

h You cannot refuse to give someone a job just because of their age. It's considered **discrimination** (n).

2 Choose a phrase from 1 to complete sentences a–h.

a She felt it was a case of sexual _____ when she did not get the job.

b In the past, a job for life was common, and _____ was rarely a concern.

c The _____ for women used to be 60 in the UK.

d The job pays a _____ of £15 per hour.

e In customer service, good _____ are essential.

f People who are not satisfied with their job often think about when they will _____ .

g Five people left, so we had to _____ replacements.

h I want to take a _____ next year. I'm planning to travel for a year and luckily my company will keep my job open for me.

3 Ask a partner's opinion. Use vocabulary in 1 and 2.

- Would you ever take a career break?
- Is it ever OK to discriminate by age?
- How important is job security to you?

B | Personal qualities

These words/phrases can all be used to describe personal qualities.

1 Look at comments a–h from an interview. Match the words in *italics* to definitions 1–8.

a 'My *maturity* allows me to base my decisions on a lot of experience and to make a sensible decision.' ___

b 'Ten years in customer service means I have *a wealth of experience* relevant to this role.' ___

c 'It is essential to create a good *rapport* with your staff when managing a team.' ___

d 'I work extremely hard and meet all my deadlines. I'm a very *conscientious* worker.' ___

e 'I feel very positive and *enthusiastic* about taking on this new role. It's the ideal job for me.' ___

f 'I have often been put in charge of important projects as I've always been considered *reliable*.' ___

g 'I am a good sales person largely because I am *determined* to meet my targets.' ___

h 'I can work individually but I'm also a good *team player* and able to work towards common goals.' ___

1 wanting something very much (adj)
2 being mentally and emotionally like an adult (n)
3 a lot of knowledge or skills from doing something (n)
4 taking care and putting a lot of effort into your work (adj)
5 good at working in a group (n)
6 a good understanding of someone and the ability to communicate well with them (n)
7 someone who can be trusted or believed because they work in a way that you expect (adj)
8 showing a lot of energy and interest (adj)

2 Choose one quality from 1 that you think is key for the jobs below. Explain your reasons in pairs.

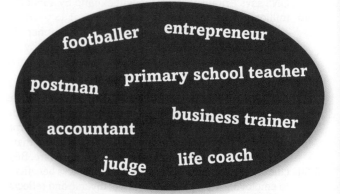

footballer   entrepreneur

postman   primary school teacher

accountant   business trainer

judge   life coach

3 Which three qualities from the list in 1 would you be most likely to use to describe yourself in an application for a job?

Writing skills

Drafting is an important part of the writing process. You can use many of the skills practised in this book to develop a first draft. You can also use a list of these skills to recheck what you have written.

A | Using a checklist to write a draft

Work in pairs. You are planning a 500 word essay.

1 Number steps a–h from the start (1) to the end (8) of the essay writing process.

   a plan your essay _____
   b write a first draft _____
   c analyse the question _____
   d develop research questions _____
   e brainstorm your ideas _____
   f proofread your writing _____
   g conduct your research _____
   h organize your ideas _____

2 Read the essay title. Identify the parts in the title.

> Discuss the benefits for companies of the changes in the average age of the workforce in the UK.

the instruction   the focus   the topic   the limitation

3 Prepare your ideas for the essay. Brainstorm ideas and organize them into:

   • an introduction
   • two main paragraphs
   • a conclusion

4 Plan your research questions.

   • What additional information do you need that is not included in the text on page 65?
   • Where will you look for the extra information?

5 In which part of the essay would you expect to include features a–g, in the introduction (I), in a main paragraph (P) or in the conclusion (C)?

   a a topic sentence _____
   b a summary of the main ideas _____
   c an indication of the essay's structure _____
   d a thesis statement showing the main argument or point of view _____
   e paragraph transition sentences _____
   f supporting details _____
   g a restatement of the thesis _____

6 Think about your main idea for each paragraph.

   a What ideas do you have to support your main idea?
   b Look at the text again. Could you use the text to support any of your main ideas? Underline any possible part you could use.
   c If you can use part of the text, explain to your partner how you think it supports the main idea.

B | Using a checklist to revise writing

Work in pairs. You are preparing to write a 500 word essay.

1 Look at three checklists for different parts of an essay. Which part of the essay does each set match to? Write 'Introduction', 'Paragraph' or 'Conclusion'.

   Set A _____
   • Is there a topic sentence?
   • Does everything relate to the main idea?
   • Do the examples clearly and logically support the main idea?
   • Is there a summary, conclusion or transition?

   Set B _____
   • Does it catch the reader's interest?
   • Does it move from general to specific?
   • Does it give a clear outline of the structure of the essay?
   • Does it indicate a clear line of argument?

   Set C _____
   • Is there a summary or logical drawing together of ideas?
   • Is no new information mentioned?
   • Is the thesis of the essay clearly restated?

2 Brainstorm and list other things you should check at the drafting stage.

   1 *word formation*

Writing task

Use your research questions from A4 to look into your essay topic further. Then complete your plan for the essay and write at least 500 words on the topic. Use checklists to check and revise your drafts.

Answer key

Unit 1 Communication

Reading strategies

A | Predicting content

1 Suggested answer: Explaining the meaning of 'perception' and how it influences the way people communicate.
2 **Figure 1.1** = an old lady/a young lady/both
  Figure 1.2 = a goblet/two faces/both
  Figure 1.3 = the number 13/letter B/both/some dots
3 Suggested answer: They demonstrate that different people perceive the same thing in different ways.

B | Reading closely for detailed information

1 **A** We give our own meaning to shapes, sounds, etc. The words we use, the way we look and our body language communicate our view of the world to other people.
  B We analyse and judge information from the world around us.
  C Our language is part of the culture we experience and provides the descriptive labels for this culture.
  D By not saying 'please', because in their language 'please' is not a separate word.
  E In the UK speech is suggestive and idiomatic. In the USA it is 'normal' to explain all details clearly and directly. In France, ambiguity and subtlety are expected; much is communicated by what is not said.
2 **a** 3   **b** 1   **c** 2   **d** 4

Business vocabulary

A | Noun collocations

1 **a** 1   **b** 2   **c** 1
2 **a** <u>Effective relationships</u> – Relationships that are effective
  b <u>management team</u> – The team responsible for management
  c <u>reducing costs</u> – which reduce the costs
3 **a** adjective + noun   **b** noun + noun   **c** verb + noun
4 **a** Individual differences affect how we perceive the world.
  b The team leader had little impact on the project's success.
  c The company must address the needs of its target markets.
  d We work well with our clients now because we have a shared understanding of what we want to achieve.

B | Preposition collocations

1 **a** 2   **b** 2   **c** 1
2 **a** of   **b** to   **c** on   **d** of   **e** of   **f** of

Writing skills

A | Taking notes from a text

1 No, the main meaning stays the same.
2 Suggested answers:
  Abbreviations: diff., info., org., mgr, Dept, mgement, individ.
  Key content words: individuals, perception, behaviour, interpretations, reasonable, request, unreasonable, control, objection, efficiency
  Simplifying complex sentences: Interpretations 1–4 are simplified complex sentences.
3 Suggested answers: **a** lang.   **b** ldr   **c** undstng
  d proc.   **e** comm.

4 Suggested answers:
  a Perception, mental, function, significance, stimuli, perceived, develop, help, view, world, etc. They are mostly adjectives, nouns and verbs.
  b All sentences could be shortened.
5 Suggested answers:
  Paragraph C
  LANG. = imp in world perception
  Lang labels envt + guides thinking
  e.g. Inuit 13 words 4 snow
  Cult. diffs. relevant = show influence social learning
  Paragraph D
  LANG. reflects + shapes EXPERIENCE
  influences relationships
  e.g. X 'please' offends some pple
  Paragraph E
  COMMUNICATION = how words said + silences
  UK spch = suggestive + idiomatic
  US spch = explicit + direct
  Fr. spch = ambiguity + subtlety (silnc. imp.)

B | Expanding notes

1 **a** T   **b** F   **c** T
2 **a** *analyse and judge info. received*
    We analyse and judge information we receive.
  b *PERCEPTION = key in org. behaviour*
    Perception is key in organizational behaviour.
  c *e.g. email to mgr on overtime in Dept > 4 interpretations –*
    For example, an email to managers on overtime in a department could be interpreted in four different ways.
  d *1 reasonable request – improved staffing*
    It's a reasonable request and could lead to improved levels of staffing.
  e *2 unreasonable – mgement want more control*
    It is an unreasonable request and management simply want more control.
  f *3 no objection – suspicious why*
    I have no objections but I am suspicious why the request has been made.
  g *4 +ve – reduced costs + improved efficiency*
    I'm positive about this request and think it could lead to reduced costs and improved efficiency.
  h *individ experience = diff. perception*
    Individual experiences lead to different perceptions.

Unit 2 Motivation

Reading strategies

A | Understanding main ideas

1 Victor H. Vroom
2 Introductory paragraph, three main sections (Effort-performance expectancy, Performance-outcome expectancy, Valence), final paragraph
3 1 **E** (Valence)   2 **C** (Performance-outcome expectancy)
  3 **B** (Effort-performance expectancy)
4 **a** a motivation theory   **b** before
  c one combined judgement
5 1 **C**   2 **E**   3 **D**   4 **B**

B | Understanding key phrases
1 time, money
2 'results', and in this case, 'rewards'.
Examples of positive outcomes: a bonus, a promotion, permission to leave early, a feeling of accomplishment
Examples of negative outcomes: loss of leisure time, disruption to family time
3 'extrinsic rewards': rewards provided by others, e.g. awards, promotion
'intrinsic rewards': internal experiences, e.g. a feeling of challenge, a sense of achievement
4 value

C | Interpreting graphically presented data
1 a Figure 1 (the flow chart) gives an overview of the theory.
  b Figure 2 (the table) relates to a specific section of the text.
2 1 C   2 B   3 A
3 b

Business vocabulary

| Word formation: common endings
1 Suggested answers:
Noun: -tion -age -ance -ancy -ence -er -ism -ity -ment -ness -ship -sion
Verb: -ate -fy -ise
Adjective: -al -able -ant -ed -ful -ive -ous
Adverb: -ly
2 a performance b quickly c environmental
  d permission e accomplishment f negative
  g willingness h motivate
3 performance (n) quickly (adv) environmental (adj)
  permission (n) accomplishment (n) negative (adj)
  willingness (n) motivate (v)
4 accomplish (v) assessment (n) environmentally (adv)
  expectation (n) motivational (adj) negatively (adv)
  perform (v) permit (v)
5 a expect b motivate c environment
  d performing e permitted f accomplished
6 a unmotivated b accomplishments c performance
  d environmentally e expectation f permission

Writing skills

A | Preparing for summary writing
1 a T b F c F d T e F f F g T
2 a Departments b Transport c Leaders
  d Jobs/Professions
3 non-content words
4 Suggested answers:
  1 With performance-outcome expectancy we assess the probability that our successful performance will lead to certain outcomes.
  2 Rewards that are related to our own internal experiences with successful performance, such as feelings of achievement, challenge, and growth, are known as intrinsic rewards.
  3 However, the value of possible negative outcomes, such as the loss of free time or the effect on our family, may offset the value of rewards in a given situation.

5 Suggested answers:
  1 With performance-outcome expectancy we assess the probability that our successful performance will lead to certain outcomes.
  2 Rewards that are related to our own internal experiences with successful performance, such as feelings of achievement, challenge, and growth, are known as intrinsic rewards.
  3 However, the value of possible negative outcomes, such as the loss of free time or the effect on our family, may offset the value of rewards in a given situation.
6 Suggested answers:
  1 Performance-outcome expectancy is about evaluating how good performance will lead to specific results.
  2 Rewards connected to personal feelings of success and development are called intrinsic rewards.
  3 Bad results such as no spare time may cancel out the positives.

B | Using topic sentences
1 B ✓ C ✓ D ✓ E ✓
  A This is the topic of text rather than of the paragraph.
  F This is not a clear topic sentence, as it is concluding the text.
5 Suggested answer:
(A) Vroom's theory says that motivation consists of three stages. (B) Stage 1 (Effort-Performance) is about whether effort results in appropriate performance. (C) Stage 2 (Performance-Outcome) is about evaluating how good performance will result in rewards. (D) There are monetary and non-monetary kinds of reward, and rewards can be both from others or from a feeling of personal satisfaction. (E) Stage 3 is about the expected value to you of a reward. (F) The theory says that people assess the three stages then make one judgement.

Unit 3 The future of management

Reading strategies

A | Identifying general point of view
1 c
2 A F   B T   C T   D F   E F   F F   G F
  H T

B | Identifying detailed point of view
A But I believe a more useful approach is to reinvent management – to go back to basic principles of what management is all about.
B management simply involves getting people to come together to achieve goals that they could not achieve on their own.
C these objectives are not what drives success in most sectors today
D We all need to be leaders and managers: we need to be able to influence others through our ideas, words, and actions, and we also need to be able to get work done through others on a day-to-day basis.
E Management is fundamentally about how individuals work together, and the basic laws of social interaction are not open to dramatic change.
F But management practices are largely dependent on context, and as the nature of business organizations evolves, so too will management.
G We need to develop a more detailed understanding of what management is about to make better choices.
H Alas, there is no recipe book for reinventing management.

69

C | Reacting to the text

1 Suggested answers:
LEADER: *to innovate*, to influence, to set direction, to manage change, to motivate people
MANAGER: *to budget*, to improve efficiency, to plan, to organize, to be responsible for quality control, to get people together to accomplish desired goals, to get work done on a day-to-day basis

Business vocabulary

A | 'Management' and 'leadership'

1, 2

a standardization (noun) – the process of making everything similar
b hierarchy (noun) – the structure/different levels within a company
c to plan (verb) – to decide how you are going to do something
d to budget (verb) – to plan financially
e to organize (verb) – to make arrangements
f to control (verb) – to tell someone what to do
g to manage change (verb) – to oversee and control a transition
h to motivate (verb) – to make someone want to do something well
i individual traits (adjective + plural noun) – the particular characteristics of a person
j individual style (adjective + noun) – the particular method or manner of a person
k to influence others (verb) – to have an effect on other people

3 a plan   b style   c control   d manage change
e hierarchy   f Bureaucracy

4 Suggested answers: **Leadership**: b, d   **Management**: a, c, e, f

B | Change

1 **Big change:** to change noticeably, to reinvent, a whole new model
Little change: a minor development, a small shift
Movement forwards: to move on, to progress, a step forward
Movement backwards: to go back to basics

2 a minor developments/small shifts
b to go back to basics
c change management noticeably OR reinvent management
d step forward

Writing skills

A | Analysing questions

1 [Examine] = c Instruction [the changes in] = b Focus [IBM's corporate strategy] = a Main topic [in Europe] = d Limitation.
2 Adding each part makes the topic of the question more specific.
3 a [Discuss] = Instruction [Kotter's theories of leadership] = Topic.
b [Compare and contrast] = Instruction [the management style of IBM and Google] = Topic [in the 1990s] = Limitation.
c [Analyse] = Instruction [the changes] = Focus [in leadership style] = Topic [during the last century] = Limitation.
d ['Management' is bureaucratic, 'leadership' is inspirational] = Topic [To what extent do you agree?] = Instruction.
e [Define] = Instruction ['management'] = Topic [indicating] = Instruction [its general scope and function] = Focus.

f [Analyse] (= Instruction) [the differences] (= Focus) [in leadership style] (= Topic) [between the USA and Japan] (= Limitation).

B | Understanding instructions

1 The main difference is that question a would not require any opinion whereas question b would.
2 a 4   b 2   c 3   d 5   e 6   f 1

C | Developing research questions

1 Suggested answers: What was the theory based on? How does this theory relate to other leadership theories? What criticisms have been made of this theory by other scholars?
2 Suggested answers:
Examine the changes in IBM's corporate strategy in Europe. What is IBMs corporate strategy? How did IBM start? How has its origins influenced its strategy? What clear stages of development are there in IBM's history? Has its strategy changed or is it largely the same? Is its strategy in Europe different?, etc.
Analyse the changes in leadership style during the last century. How is leadership defined? How has leadership changed? What theories of leadership are there? Does leadership only change with time or are there other influences on change?, etc.

Unit 4 Marketing

Reading strategies

A | Understanding a text using background knowledge

5 Suggested answers for 2–4:
2 By using a product portfolio matrix.
3, 4 All characteristics are important; it is the correct balance of types of product that is most important.

B | Understanding the relationship between text and graphic

1 a An overview of the product portfolio theory.
b The diagram is difficult to interpret, and needs to be looked at in relation to the text.
2 a Paragraph **B**.
b How the matrix measure products, an explanation of the meaning of the graph axes and categories.
3 a Yes, as 4.2 simply shows the future position.
b It tells us the limitations of the graph.

C | Finding support for an opinion

1 Support from the text:
A What is really important is an understanding of the performance of a company's products relative to each other.
B The success of a product is based on two key variables, market growth and relative market share.
C In some industries a market growth rate of 5 per cent is regarded as high, whereas in others this might be 10 per cent.
D Stars are probably market leaders, but their growth has to be financed through fairly heavy levels of investment.
E Dogs should only be retained as long as they contribute to positive cash flow and do not restrict the use of assets and resources elsewhere in the business.
F An unbalanced portfolio is one that has too many products grouped in one or two quadrants.
G However, the Boston Box only provides strategic indicators, not solutions.

Business vocabulary

A | Marketing

1 1 c 2 f 3 b 4 a 5 d 6 e 7 g

B | Verb–preposition collocations

1, 2 a on b to c on d in e to f by g to
   h on

3 1 b to refer to
  2 a to base (something) on
  3 h to plot (something) on
  4 c to depend on
  5 d to exist in
  6 f to be generated by
  7 e to draw attention to
  8 g to contribute to

4 a based on b depends on c referred to
  d exists in e contribute to f generated by
  g draw attention to h plotted on

Writing skills

A | Paraphrasing sentences

1 The meaning is the same but the language is different. Sentence A is from the text.
2 1 When managing = responsible for the management of
  2 it is important to realize = it is essential to recognize
  3 understanding = An understanding of
  4 an individual product = a single product
  5 can often fail to give the complete picture = won't necessarily tell you everything you need to know
3 Word order, vocabulary and grammar have changed.
4 The words that have not changed are words that are central to the theory, e.g. *portfolio of products*, *performance*.
5 2 is the best paraphrase: word order, grammar and vocabulary have changed, BUT terms central to the theory, and the meaning, have not changed.
6 Suggested answers:
  a When a company's product exists in a falling market it is essential that the company recognizes this.
  b Knowing what a rival company is doing should be a priority for a company wherever possible.
  c It is best practice to do a portfolio analysis when a company is facing financial challenges.

B | Writing practice

1 Suggested answer: Understanding how to move financial resources to achieve maximum performance, paying attention to cash flow and the make-up of a company's products, can be achieved through portfolio analysis.
2 Suggested answer: Unequal distribution of products in one or two areas in a portfolio means that it is not balanced; a portfolio that is spread evenly across the matrix can be described as being in a good financial position.

Unit 5 Management systems

Reading strategies

A | Reading for general understanding

1 1841 – the year Fayol was born
2 1860 – the year Fayol joined the mining company Commentry-Fourchambault-Decazeville

3 1888 – the year Fayol became managing director of the company
4 1949 – the year Fayol's book became widely available in English
5 14 – the number of key ideas in Fayol's principles of management
6 19 – the age Fayol graduated as the best student of his year in engineering
7 1918 – the year Fayol retired
8 1925 – the year Fayol died

B | Understanding main and supporting ideas

1 a
2 a
3 a the background to the development of the theory
  b a description of the 14 key principles of the theory
4 B = more explanation; C = examples and/or explanation

C | Critical reading

1 Suggested answers: **Roles**: 1, 2, 10 **Control/power**: 2, 3, 4, 5, 8, 9 **Rewards for staff**: 7, 12 **Equality**: 6, 11
3 The use of *however* to contrast with what has just been stated, and the word *limits*, which highlights restrictions around the principle he has described.
4 a In the text, Fayol makes few further comments and no criticisms.
  b Suggested answers:
  2 This potentially limits creativity and contradicts point 13.
  3 Perhaps not everyone needs to be disciplined; this may cause frustration.
  4 Is this practical? Many people have several roles with a line manager for each.
  5 In large organizations, it is not always realistic or possible to have one head.
  6 If individual interests are not taken into consideration staff retention may be affected.
  7 Is this possible? Staff usually want more and the company want to pay less.
  8 Centralization or decentralization might be economically necessary regardless of the quality of the staff.
  9 Especially for major decisions, superiors must not be left out.
  10 In today's world, with multiple locations, suppliers and manufacturers, this is unrealistic. It is not always possible to have capable people in all the right positions.
  11 Not all good managers are friendly or fair.
  12 A certain level of threat could motivate staff to work harder to keep their jobs?
  13 Delegating initiative can mean losing control (see point 2).
  14 A degree of conflict can be stimulating as well, making people think twice about how, when and why things should be done.

Business vocabulary

| Noun combinations to define or describe

1 a 2 b 3 c 1
2 It is largely descriptive, with a small element of evaluation.
3 1 management 2 work 3 business
  4 initiative 5 the manager 6 superiors
  7 unemployment 8 strength
4 a share of initiative b division of work
  c threat of unemployment d source of strength
  e operation of business f chain of superiors
  g ideas of management h character of the manager

Writing skills

A | Paragraph structure
1 1 d   2 a   3 c   4 b
2 c, a, d, b

B | Transitioning between paragraphs
1 The sentence ends with a phrase (*…, and this can be achieved in a number of ways.*) which transitions from the current paragraph to the next paragraph of the text.
2 The next paragraph is likely to contain theories and/or examples of how management can make informed decisions about levels of pay.

Unit 6 Ethics

Reading strategies

A | Understanding a text using headings
1 a 3 Corporate responsibility as a moral obligation
  b 2 The Friedmanite position
  c 1 Positioning corporate responsibility
2 1 C   2 B   3 E   4 D
3 a F   b T   c F   d T   e T

B | Predicting content using topic sentences
3 G a T   b F
  H a F   b T
  I a T   b F
  J a F   b T
  K a F   b T

Business vocabulary

| Noun collocations
1 1 c   2 a   3 g   4 b   5 e   6 f   7 d
2 a economic interests   b finance director
  c management policies   d sales target
  e education system   f HR department
  g human welfare

Writing skills

A | Describing similarity and difference
1 Conversely, Similarly, However
2 **Expressing similarity**: Similarly
  Expressing difference: Conversely, However
3 a Conversely,/However,   b In the same way,/Similarly,
  c However,   d In the same way,/Similarly,
4 is the same as
5 **Expressing similarity**: x is like, the same as, both x and y are … **Expressing difference**: different from, x is …, whereas y is …, in contrast, on the one hand … on the other hand
7 a the same as, like   b different from   c both
  d compared with, whereas

Unit 7 Decision-making

Reading strategies

A | Reading quickly for general understanding
1 c
2 non-rational
3 1 the Satisficing model   2 the Garbage Can model
  3 the Incremental model   4 the Rational model

B | Identifying the writer's point of view
1 a F   b T   c F   d F
2 Suggested answers:
  Rational model: Strength – the rational view is useful in providing a benchmark against which to compare actual managerial decision-making patterns Weakness – the difficulties of getting perfect information and making 'optimal' decisions
  Satisficing model: Strength – a good decision-making approach when the cost of delaying a decision or searching for a better alternative is greater than the reward from following such an approach Weakness – managers sometimes make a habit of using the simple satisficing approach even in situations where the cost of searching for further alternatives is justified given the possible gain
  Incremental model: Strength – aimed at short-term easing of a problem Weakness – in the long run, incremental decisions may prove not to work
  Garbage Can model: Strength – can sometimes lead managers to take advantage of unforeseen opportunities Weakness – can also lead to severe problems from which it may be difficult to recover in complex situations
3 Usually the strength is mentioned first followed by the weakness. This structure is used when the writer wants to emphasize the weaknesses more than the strengths; generally the writer thinks that these are poor models for decision-making.
4 Suggested answer: 1 Satisficing   2 Incremental
                        3 Garbage Can   4 Rational
  Overall the Rational model seems to be least effective, according to the writer.

C | Reading closely for detailed information
1 That they are making decisions in the best economic interests of the firm.
2 Because it is very difficult to get perfect information to inform such a decision.
3 A study of the actual behaviours of managers in making decisions.
4 Managers get into the habit of making the simplest/easiest decision.
5 Because they are making the smallest response possible to reduce the problem to a manageable level.
6 A homeowner who uses extension cables instead of installing extra electric power points; in the long run, the electricity supply will fail.
7 The people that happen to be involved, the problems they happen to be concerned with at the time, the opportunities they happen to find and the solutions they tend to favour.
8 He failed to operate within a reasonably defined strategy and tried to diversify the business, but it failed.

Business vocabulary

A | Decision-making
1 a 1   b 5   c 4   d 2   e 3   f 6
2 1 complex situations   2 optimal decisions
  3 economic theory   4 economic behaviour
  5 serious flaws   6 decision-making patterns

B | Adjective–noun collocations

1 1 relative importance   2 possible gain
   3 long-term goals   4 random pattern
   5 desirable outcome   6 defined strategy
2 a defined strategy   b relative importance
   c possible gains   d desirable outcome
   e long-term goals   f random patterns

Writing skills

B | Organizing ideas

1 a In the centre: Rational decision-making
   b Origins of model, Definition of model, Weaknesses
   c Ideas from the reading text are underlined in the ideas map; the others are extra ideas.
     Note: Main headings and additional notes developed through brainstorming and mind-mapping process.

Unit 8 Increasing productivity

Study focus

1 *productivity* = the amount of output an employee produces
performance = the way an employee carries out their role in a company or workplace

Reading strategies

A | Reading for general understanding

A 2   B 2   C 2   D 1   E 2

B | Reading closely for detailed information

A 1 The one that produces 10 pairs of shoes per day for the same labour cost.
   2 They could price low to increase volume, or price high to get a higher profit margin.
B 3 The machines were not as efficient as they hoped, and less flexible than a human workforce.
   4 They can run the machines for longer, maintain them carefully to prevent breakdowns, improve how the machines are operated.
C 5 Trained staff produce more, make fewer mistakes, work more quickly and require less supervision.
   6 The higher costs of training and disruption to work flow.
D 7 To create circumstances in which people want to do their job.
   8 The two examples of motivation.
E 9 Through well-organized work, effective people management and the coordination of resources.
   10 To increase productivity by 10% every year until they had beaten the market-leading firm.

C | Reacting to the text

• The four methods of improving productivity are the titles of sections B, C, D and E.

Business vocabulary

A | Pronoun referents

1 a It   b The output per employee
2 a a firm, the price   b robotic production lines
   c achieving productivity gains without new equipment
   d most people
3 1 productivity   2 companies   3 productivity
   4 profitability   5 productivity (i.e. the fact that productivity is key to competitiveness)   6 productivity (i.e. the fact that productivity is key to competitiveness)

B | 'Production' or 'productivity'?

1 Suggested answers: *Production* is the process of making something. *Productivity* is the rate at which something is produced in relation to the number of people or resources used to produce it.
2 a production   b productivity   c production
   d production   e productivity
3 a production   b activities   c sensitivity   d creations

Writing skills

A | Expanding an idea with reasons and examples

1 a 1 The output per employee is a very important measure of a firm's performance.
     2 By increasing productivity a firm can improve its competitiveness.
   b 1 is supported by a reason, 2 is supported by an example
2 a because   b For example
3 In 2, the two sentences are joined by linking words *for example/because* which lead to support for the main idea.
4 **Example**: by way of illustration, for instance, in the case of, … shows this point clearly, such as
   Reason: as a result of, because, due to (the fact that), since
5 Suggested answers: a for instance   b due to
   c shows this point clearly   d as a result of/due to
   e such as, For instance
6 General rules: Use a comma after *for example, … for instance, … by way of illustration, …* Use a comma before *such as … due to (the fact that) … as a result of … because …* when these expressions begin the second part of a sentence. Use capital letters and a following comma when these expressions start the second sentence. *By way of illustration, … For instance, … In the case of …, As a result of …, Due to …,* can all start a sentence. Use *… shows this point clearly.*, followed by a full stop, at the end of a sentence.

B | Writing practice

Suggested example for each:
1 …, as a result of their lack of motivation.
2 …, due to the fact that it can increase productivity.
3 … . For example, it may increase staff motivation and consequently productivity.
4 …, since it will impact on many aspects of the business's success.

Unit 9 Job satisfaction

Reading strategies

A | Reading quickly for specific information

1 a 5
   b 1 individual factors   2 environmental factors
     3 cultural factors   4 social factors
     5 organizational factors
   c 4
   d 1 meaninglessness   2 powerlessness
     3 self-estrangement   4 isolation

B | Identifying point of view

1 **a** LJ Mullins   **b** Charles Handy   **c** the Chartered Management Institute
2 **a** the author, Mullins
   b a management expert, Charles Handy
   c the Chartered Management Institute, in their 2003 study
   d the Chartered Management Institute, in their 2003 study
3 **a** 2   **b** 2 and 3

Business vocabulary

A | Research and data

1 **a** quantitative   **b** qualitative
2 1 quantitative   2 qualitative
3 quantitative data (*nearly half of …/sizable numbers*)
4 **a**
5 1
6 **a** to undertake   **b** to survey   **c** A questionnaire
   d an interview   **e** to investigate   **f** A random sample

B | Connection and relationship

1 **a** with   **b** of   **c** by   **d** to   **e** in   **f** to   **g** to
   h from
2 **a** associated with   **b** consists of   **c** approach to
   d affected by   **e** stems from   **f** relating to
   g result in   **h** refers to

Writing skills

A | Referencing and citation

1 **a** work performance is closely linked to the quality of the workplace
   b The year of publication of the book or article in which this idea appeared.
   c It summarizes the supporting opinion of an expert in the field.
2 **a** 'a wide range of variables relating to individual, social, cultural, organisational and environmental factors.'
   b The year of publication and page number.
   c It demonstrates the supporting opinion of an expert in the field.
3 **a** 1
   b They are put in quotation marks.
   c When it is difficult to explain the idea in another way because it is expressed so succinctly, OR when the quote is very well known.
4 1 claims   2 states   3 demonstrates
5 **a** demonstrates   **b** states   **c** claims
6 **Neutral**: defines, describes, states
   For: acknowledges, asserts, maintains
   Against: contends, cautions, disputes

B | Writing practice
Suggested answers:
1 Mullins (2007:277) claims that 'Some workers may be satisfied with certain aspects of their work and dissatisfied with other aspects.'
2 Mullins (2007) demonstrates that job satisfaction now has closer links to general issues such as the design of jobs, work organization and quality issues including stress management and work-life balance.

Unit 10 New business

Reading strategies

A | Reading quickly for general understanding

1 b
2 Introduction = paragraph **A**
   Main part = paragraph **B**
   Conclusion = paragraph **C**
3 1 c   2 f   3 d   4 e   5 b   6 a

B | Understanding main and supporting ideas

1 b
2 **a** 5 The growth rate of the industry
   b 1 Minimum efficient scale
   c 3 The overall rate of innovation in the firm's industry
   d 4 The rate of innovation among small firms in the firm's industry
   e 6 Whether the firm is a multi-plant operation
   f 2 The start-up size of firm
3 b

Business vocabulary

A | Challenge

1 *to be affected by* (*a problem*) = a problem is having an impact on something; *to overcome* (*a problem*) = to deal with a problem
2 **to be presented with a challenge**: to be affected by, to be confronted by, to be faced by, to be threatened by
   to handle a challenge: to deal with, to overcome, to rise above, to tackle
4 **a** to tackle   **b** to be confronted by   **c** to rise above
5 **a** was affected by   **b** was threatened by

B | Measurements and amounts

1 **a** 4   **b** 1   **c** 6   **d** 5   **e** 2   **f** 8   **g** 3   **h** 7
2 **a** sample   **b** average/mean   **c** average
   d overall   **e** majority   **f** minority
   g proportion/percentage   **h** proportion/percentage

Writing skills

A | Writing introductions and conclusions

1 b, d, a, c
2 Sentence c
3 Sentence b
4 new ideas or information
5 Suggested answers:
   a The manufacturing sector forms the basis of a number of growing economies.
   b The web is the main place new companies start.
   c The maximum time most new companies survive is five years.
   d Small companies particularly rely on customer loyalty.
   e A lack of market knowledge is the reason many companies fail.
6 Suggested answers:
   a A company with one location will be confronted by less risk than firms trading in a number of locations.
   b New companies have to deal with greater risks when entering a sector where businesses are already efficient.
   c Markets with little innovation will be easier to tackle than very innovative markets.
   d A good business strategy will have a more positive impact on a new company's success than a poorly developed plan.

Unit 11 The impact of IT

Reading strategies

A | Understanding a text using background knowledge
4 *Internet* = the system of connected computers around the world
intranet = a system like the internet but limited internally to a company
extranet = a computer system to connect organizations and allow them to communicate

B | Reading closely for detailed information
Suggested answers:
1 The telephone is no longer only about communicating by voice: fibre optic cables have increased capacity and reduced cost so now more data can be passed more cheaply and over long distances between devices like mobiles and computers.
2 Television has been changed by communications satellites, which created the effect of a 'global community', and by digital technology, which resulted in more TV channels and the potential convergence of TV and computers.
3 The networked computer has become much smaller and more powerful through the increasing power of the microchip, and is now embedded in multiple gadgets.
4 TCP/IP has provided a common language through which data can be sent over the Internet, so that difference devices can be part of a single network; mobile/wireless technology has freed the computer from the desktop so that information can be accessed from anywhere.

C | Understanding the relationship between text and graphic
1 Stage 1 c   Stage 2 a   Stage 3 e   Stage 4 b   Stage 5 d
2 b In Stage 5, businesses have direct links to their customers rather than only internally or between businesses.
4 Suggested answers:
a **Information** is 'static': customers look at information on a company's website; suppliers use their website to show customers what they offer; customers can compare between suppliers
Interaction is 'interactive': customers input information/ questions about a product or service; the system uses the customer information (e.g. preferred dates and times of travel) to respond about availability and price
Transaction is 'active': customers buy products or services and get them delivered through a website; suppliers can agree electronically to meet a purchase order
Integration is 'linked together': a company's information systems and those of its suppliers and customers converge to create an e-system. The text provides additional examples, e.g. Dell Computing.
b **Transformation** (= change of state): the business no longer operates in a traditional sense and is purely run and managed at all stages through a portal such as the Internet

Business vocabulary

| New ideas
1 a adopted (line 20)   b launch (line 21)
  c breakthrough (line 23) d invention (line 38)
2 1 a   2 d   3 b   4 c
3 a breakthroughs/advances   b embrace/adopt
  c launch/unveiling   d invention/innovation

Writing skills

A | SKILLS REVIEW Synthesizing
1 d, a, c, b
2 a A quote can come at any point in a paragraph but often comes as a support to the main idea so is commonly the second sentence.
  b The first sentence introduces the main idea and possibly leads into the quote. The sentences that follow comment on the significance of the point the quote makes, either supporting it or arguing with it.
3 **For**: to assert, to contend, to maintain   **Against**: to caution, to dispute   **Neutral**: to acknowledge, to define, to describe, to state
4 a A direct quote uses the exact words of the author. An indirect quote uses the ideas of the author expressed in a different way.
  b A direct quote includes the author's surname, the year of publication (followed by a colon) and the page number in brackets, and quotation marks around the exact words. An indirect quote includes the author's surname, and the year of publication in brackets.
5 a According to Boddy (2007:383), 'Linking mobile phones to the Internet has led to the explosive growth of the "Wireless Internet".'
  b Boddy (2007) states that connecting mobile devices to the Internet has resulted in significant growth in the 'Wireless Internet'.
6 a summarizing   b summarizing   c paraphrasing
  d paraphrasing
7 The key changes are grammar, vocabulary and word order.

B | Writing practice
1 Suggested answer:
Traditional customer research methods can be slow, whereas IT communities allow a company to understand customers well, and to find out how products or services can be made better.
2 Suggested answers:
• Technology has changed the way modern companies conduct business. Boddy (2007) states that technological developments, along with the changing politics of the world, have rapidly expanded many companies' customer base. However, whilst it may have opened up larger markets, this does not mean businesses can always successfully operate in these. Companies need to invest a lot of time and resources into developing their products to meet individual market needs.
• Technology has changed the way modern companies conduct business. According to Boddy (2007:384) it is 'creating a wider, often global, market for many goods and services'. However, whilst it may have opened up larger markets, this does not mean businesses can always successfully operate in these. Companies need to invest a lot of time and resources into developing their products to meet individual market needs.

Unit 12 Dealing with change

Reading strategies

A | Reading quickly for specific information

1 **Current problems**: Mergers/acquisitions, Organizational decline/revitalization, Conflict management
OD activities: Team-building activities, Survey-feedback activities, Large group interventions

2 1 Team-building activities 2 Survey-feedback activities
  3 Mergers/acquisitions
  4 Organizational decline/revitalization
  5 Conflict management 6 Large group interventions

B | Reading closely for detailed information

1 To plan change, paying particular attention to people and relationships, in order to make a company more effective and more able to adapt to change in the future.

2 a Because of the failure of executives to determine whether the administrative style and corporate culture of each company are a good fit.
  b By managing conflicts, fostering commitment and facilitating communication.
  c A combination of strong-willed individuals failing to agree, different priorities, personal dislikes.
  d They need to focus on broader issues such as encouraging a sense of community, building trust and making opportunities for personal growth.
  e It can enhance cohesiveness, improve communication skills and help focus on common goals.
  f OD consultants meet with groups to provide feedback about the problems that have been identified.
  g People from all parts of an organization, stakeholders in change.
  h It allows fundamental large-scale change to happen quickly.

C | Identifying the writer's point of view

1 a

2 a Large group interventions
  b The author use expressions which emphasize the power and effectiveness of the OD approach, and contrasts it favourably with the alternative, incremental approach to change management: 'The acceleration of change when the entire system is involved can be quite remarkable. In addition, learning occurs across all parts of the organization simultaneously, rather than in individuals, small groups, or business units. The result is that the large-group approach offers greater possibilities for fundamental, radical transformation of the entire culture, whereas the traditional approach creates incremental change in a few individuals or small groups at a time.' (lines 107–116)

Business vocabulary

A | Ownership of a company

1 a 1 b 2 c 1 d 1

2 Suggested answers:
  a *acquisition* (n): the purchase of another company
  b *integration* (n): the combining of two or more things, in a business context with the aim of being more effective
  c *takeover* (n): when one company gains control of another by buying most of its shares
  d *joint venture* (n): when two companies work together on a project

B | Change verbs

1 a 4 b 1 c 3 d 6 e 7 f 5 g 8 h 2

2 a After the talk, I felt completely revitalized.
  b The training enabled me to deal with the situation effectively.
  c The company felt that people would enjoy being asked to participate in the project.
  d Many employees did not feel that the merger enhanced the company.
  e Our manager was very experienced at facilitating change.
  f They refused to accept the terms of the merger.
  g The company tried to encourage the public to engage in the discussion.
  h The employees resisted the changes and went on strike.

Writing skills

A | Organizing ideas

1 c, a, d, b

2 c = a statement, a = a counter opinion, d = a supporting quote, fact or explanation, b = a concluding sentence

B | Writing an argument

1 a F b O c F d O e O f F

2 **For**: as well as, furthermore, in addition, moreover
  Against: having said that, however, nevertheless, on the other hand

4 b is more cautious.

5 Suggested answers: can, could, could be possible, may, might imply that, might suggest that, tend(s) to

6 Suggested answers:
  a Mergers and acquisitions might have a negative impact on company morale.
  b It could be argued that team-building improves cohesiveness.
  c Conflict can occur in every company.
  d OD techniques tend to contribute to cultural revitalization.

C | Writing practice

1 Suggested answers:
  a Marketing campaigns might be one reason why a company is successful, however it is unlikely that there is any sole reason behind a company's success.
  b It could be argued that conflict is largely the result of poor management, on the other hand it could equally be argued that it is the working environment that is responsible.
  c Poor communication skills tend to create difficult working relationships. In addition, these poor communication skills might lead to poor customer relations.

Unit 13 Understanding the market

Reading strategies

A | Understanding main and supporting ideas

1 1 D 2 B 3 C

2 a 2 b 1 c 3 d 2 e 1 f 3

B | Reading closely for detailed information

1 a By demographics, psychology and other types of buyer-behaviour.
  b The attractiveness of the market and the company's ability to compete.

c To differentiate their product or service from that of competitors.

d Bottom-up starts with small groups of customers rather than a sector profile.

e They are in regular contact so they know their customers' needs well.

f Not usually; it often happens by accident.

C | Finding support for an opinion

a 3 supplier markets   **b** 5 referral markets

c 1 internal markets   **d** 2 recruitment markets

e 4 influence markets   **f** 6 customer markets

Business vocabulary

A | Marketing

1 b to divide

c to aim at, or try to reach

d to put something in a specific place in relation to something else

e to describe the typical features of something

f to assess the worth of something

g to make something different

h to find, choose or select

2 1 identify   **2** segment   **3** target   **4** position

5 profile   **6** define   **7** evaluate   **8** differentiate

B | Collocations with 'market'

1, 2 1 customer market   **2** recruitment market

3 referral market   **4** target market

5 market opportunity   **6** market overview

7 marketplace   **8** market position

Writing skills

A | Showing cause and effect

1 a The outcome of the recruitment strategy was a much higher qualified group of staff

b Word of mouth marketing often leads to increased sales

c Customer loyalty has increased; consequently the business is more stable.

d When a small company knows its customers well it is able to target its needs effectively.

e Small businesses survive on account of successful marketing.

2 a Since   **b** consequence   **c** owing to

d consequently/hence/so

3 Suggested answers:

a 3 Top companies often have large marketing budgets. *Consequently/For this reason/Hence/So* they often follow a top-down marketing strategy.
OR Top companies often have large marketing budgets, *hence/consequently/so* they often follow a top-down marketing strategy.

b 2 Small companies have small marketing budgets. *Accordingly/Consequently/Hence/So/For this reason* they rely on word-of-mouth recommendation.
OR Small companies have small marketing budgets, *accordingly/hence/consequently/so* they …

c 1 Small businesses often rely on trade from larger companies, and *accordingly/consequently/for this reason/hence/so* often suffer from cash flow problems due to slow payments.

d 4 Many contracts come from governments, and *accordingly/consequently/for this reason/hence/so* it is important for them to maintain good relationships with these groups.

Punctuation note: *for this reason* is the only expression in the list that cannot follow a comma at the end of the first idea; this expression must follow a full stop or colon. (NOT Small companies have small marketing budgets, for this reason they …) However, it can follow *and* (Small businesses often rely on trade from larger companies, and for this reason …)

4 a impact on   **b** precedents for   **c** outcome to
d origin of

Unit 14 Selling across cultures

Study focus

2 a red   **b** yellow   **c** green   **d** orange   **e** white
f black   **g** blue

Reading strategies

A | Predicting content using signposting

1, 2 b and d

3 1 F   **2** B   **3** H   **4** E   **5** C   **6** G   **7** D

B | Identifying the writer's point of view

1, 4, 5

Business vocabulary

A | Meaning and significance

1 1 a   **2** b   **3** b   **4** a   **5** a   **6** b   **7** b   **8** a

2 a associate   **b** means   **c** points out   **d** convey
e signifies/represents/stands for   **f** means
g signifies/represents/stands for
h signify/represent/stand for

Note: we also say *mean(s)* in contexts e, g and h, but it is a less exact word.

B | Mistakes and difficulties

1 a 4   **b** 1   **c** 5   **d** 6   **e** 7   **f** 2   **g** 3   **h** 8

2 a to learn the hard way   **b** error   **c** failed   **d** trouble
e miscalculated   **f** blundered   **g** face a problem
h costly mistake

3 a failure, a blunder, a miscalculation

Writing skills

| Understanding and using feedback

2 a The company was well represented at the conference.
b The suggestion was rejected for being inadequate.
c It was a costly error of judgement.
d The company is associated with quality products.

4 Organize the information in a logical order, e.g. statement (1), expansion of statement (2), example (3), recommendation (4). Take any statements on a different theme into a new paragraph (5). Suggested answer:

1 Colour plays a key role in the success of a product.

2 Different colours have different connotations depending on the market.

3 For example, in many cultures, the colour black represents death, yet in Iran, death is represented by the colour blue.

4 Therefore companies may need to change the colour of a product depending on their significance in the target market.

5 Companies also need to be careful when considering using the same brand name in different cultures. …

6 One of the main challenges faced by a company entering a new international market is not knowing this market well. ~~On the other hand~~ Moreover, companies need to know how to adapt their product to different markets. ~~Furthermore~~ For example, even a brand such as Coca-Cola is adapted to meet different market needs such as the sweetness of the drink. ~~Finally~~ Therefore, a successful company is likely to be one that researches the market well before entering it.

8 Reference to any of the example products from the text would provide suitable support.

Research task

Other suggestions:
Is there a summary, conclusion or transition?
Does it catch the reader's interest?
Does it move from general to specific?
Does it give a clear outline of the structure of the essay?
Does it show a clear line of argument?
Is there a clear summary or logical drawing together of ideas?
Is no new information mentioned?
Is the thesis of the essay clearly restated?

Unit 15

Reading strategies

A | Predicting content using background knowledge
3 A 2   B 2   C 2   D 2   E 2   F 1   G 2

B | Reading closely for detailed information
1 Stress is a cause of absence (lost working days).
2 Increasing.
3 They have made it a legal obligation for a company to have stress-minimizing policies.
4 Workload, change, targets and management style.
5 Overdemanding workload, lack of autonomy, poor support, low-trust work relationships, unclear roles and incomprehensible change.
6 Control over work (or autonomy).
7 The people who do the work.
8 They tend to tighten control.
9 By giving back autonomy to the people who are in contact with the customers.

C | Identifying arguments for and against
1 **Against**: 'But hang on, there's a bit of a contradiction here. Where are these pressures coming from?' (lines 22–23)
2 **For**: 'Like absence, to which it is closely related, stress doesn't need managing with yet more policies, techniques, and check-boxes.' (lines 39–41)
3 **For**: 'Research on what makes for a 'good' job invariably emphasises control over work as the number one determinant, followed by good relationships and support, a clearly understood role and security.' (lines 49–53)
4 **For**: 'Where the right psychological ingredients are in place individuals turn hard work and change into a positive challenge and opportunity for growth.' (lines 54–57)
5 **Against**: 'One of the most important qualities distinguishing 'lean' from traditional management systems is the placing of decision-making control with the people who do the work.' (lines 65–69)

6 **Against**: 'A good example is the way mobile communication devices, touted as a means of liberating people from office constraints, are in practice becoming the opposite: an additional means of surveillance which, in the words of one recent report, 'will simply translate into round-the-clock working for some employees'.' (lines 83–89)
7 **For**: 'In other words, de-stress the system, not individuals: that way everyone benefits.' (lines 104–106)

Business vocabulary

A | Dealing with problems
1 **More control**: to constrain, to tighten
   Less control: to liberate, to loosen
2 **a** to eliminate   **b** to mitigate   **c** to address
   d to oversee
3 1 overseeing   2 constraining   3 liberate   4 tighten
   5 addressed   6 eliminated
4 Suggested answers:
   a She loosened control of the team to start with to encourage creativity.
   b She had to address the problem that her team was not performing well.
   c She had to tighten control of the team because many did not perform to the right standard.
   d This change perhaps did not eliminate the problem because she tightened control too much.

B | Word formation: prefixes
1 **a** innumerable   **b** incalculable   **c** overestimate
   d incomprehensible   **e** overwhelming   **f** immeasurable
   g unmanageable   **h** unruly
2 **a** His behaviour was unmanageable.
   b My workload is overwhelming/unmanageable for me.
   c Government debts are at such a high level that they are incomprehensible for most people.
   d There are innumerable options, which is making the decision very hard.
   e The launch has been delayed by incalculable challenges.
   f They overestimated the amount of money they would make.
   g With poor leadership, employees can quickly become unruly.
   h The disastrous financial consequences of the bank's actions were immeasurable.

Writing skills

A | Problem–solution–evaluation writing
1 **a** P   **b** S   **c** E   **d** P   **e** S   **f** E
2 **Problem**: A, B, C, F   **Solution**: B, D, E, G
   Evaluation: B, D, E, G
5 **Positive**: comprehensive, efficient, fundamental, notable
   Negative: flawed, inadequate, misguided, outmoded

Unit 16 Experience

Reading strategies

A | Reading quickly for general understanding
3

B | Understanding main ideas
A 2   B 2   C 2   D 1   E 1   F 2   G 2   H 2

C | Understanding supporting ideas

1 the percentage increase in the number of employees over 60
2 the system in France and Germany, where wages rise with age
3 the expansion of the British workforce in the next 15 years
4 the proportion of B&Q's workforce that are over 50
5 the focus of older workers
6 one of the reasons why some older people work
7 something older employers have become more confident about
8 one thing promoted by the EFA (Employees Forum on Age)

Business vocabulary

A | Careers and employment

1 Suggested answers.
  a the age at which you can retire and receive a pension
  b a fixed amount of money received either hourly or weekly
  c to stop working due to the age you have reached, or
    sometimes because of ill health
  d to employ
  e a period of time away from your job
  f the group of people who work for an organization
  g how safe from losing a job someone is
  h treating people differently

2 a discrimination   b job security   c pensionable age
  d wage   e staff   f retire
  g hire   h career break

B | Personal qualities

1 a 2   b 3   c 6   d 4   e 8   f 7   g 1   h 5

Writing skills

A | Using a checklist to write a draft

1 1 c analyse the question
  2 e brainstorm your ideas
  3 h organize your ideas
  4 d develop research questions
  5 g conduct your research
  6 a plan your essay
  7 b write a first draft
  8 f proofread your writing

2 *Discuss* = the instruction
  the benefits for companies = the focus
  the changes in the average age of the workforce = the topic
  in the UK. = the limitation

5 a P   b C   c I   d I   e P   f P   g C

B | Using a checklist to revise writing

1 Set A: Paragraph
  Set B: Introduction
  Set C: Conclusion

2 Suggested answers: suitable sources, ideas supported well
  by sources, source referencing method, sentence structure,
  linking between sentences, subject–verb agreement, spelling,
  punctuation, etc.

ACKNOWLEDGEMENTS

The authors and publisher are grateful to those who have given permission to reproduce the following extracts and adaptations of copyright material: p.5 and p.37 From *Management and Organisational Behaviour 8E* by Laurie Mullins, Pearson Education Ltd. © Laurie J. Mullins, 1985, 1989, 1993, 1996, 1999, 2002, 2005, 2007. Chapters 4, 6 © Linda Carter and Laurie J. Mullins 1993, 1996, 1999, 2002, 2005, 2007. Chapter 5 © Linda Carter 1993, 1996, 1999, 2002, 2005, 2007. Chapter 17 © David Preece 1999, 2002, 2005. Reproduced by permission; pp.9–10 and pp.29–30 and pp.45–46 Extract from *Management 3E* by K. Bartol and David Martin. © 1998. Reproduced by permission of The McGraw-Hill Companies; pp.13–14 From 'The future of management: Back to basics' by Julian Birkinshaw, 17 November 2010, London Business School. Reproduced by kind permission of the author; p.17 from *Marketing* by Baines, Fill & Paige (2010) 750 words from pp.79–83. By permission of Oxford University Press; p.21 and pp.25–26 From Management: *An Introduction 4E* by David Boddy © Pearson Education Limited, 2008. Reproduced by permission; pp.34–34 Extract from *Business Studies* by Ian Marcousé. Copyright © 1999, 2003 Ian Marcousé, Andrew Gillespie, Barry Martin, Malcolm Surridge, Nancy Wall, Marie Brewer, Andrew Hammond, Ian Swift, Nigel Watson (© 1999 Clive Ruscoe). Reproduced by permission of Hodder Education; p.41 From *The Economics of Small Firms* by Peter Johnson. Copyright 2007, Routledge. Reproduced by permission of Taylor & Francis Books UK; p.49–50 From DAFT, *New Era of Management, International Edition, 2E.* © 2008 South-Western, a part of Cengage Learning, Inc. Reproduced by permission www.cengage.com/permissions; pp.53–54 From *Small Business Management and Entrepreneurship* by Leonard Stokes and Nicholas Wilson. Copyright 2006 Thomson Learning. Reproduced by permission of Cengage Learning EMEA Ltd; p.57 From Schiffman, Leon; Kanuk, Leslie *Consumer Behaviour, 9th Edition,* © 2007, pp.386–389. Reprinted by permission of Pearson Education, Inc. Upper Saddle River, NJ; p.61 From 'Get stress out of your system', by Simon Caulkin, 6 November 2005, *The Observer.* Copyright Guardian News & Media Ltd 2005. Reproduced by permission; p.65 From 'Second careers and the third age: you're only as old as your new job' by Maren Peters, 19 January 2006, *The Guardian.* Copyright Guardian News & Media Ltd 2006. Reproduced by permission.

Cover photograph by: Gareth Boden Photography

Illustrations by: Rob Briggs Roarr Design pp.9a (basic components/'Cognitive theories' in K Bartol & DC Martins, *Management*, Irwin/McGraw-Hill America 1998, pp.392–395), 9b (nonmonetary rewards/Reprinted from Bob Nelson, *1001 Ways to Reward Employees*, Workman Publishing, New York, 1994, pp.44–45), 17 (market share from B Hedley 'Strategy and the business portfolio', *Long Range Planning, 10, 1, 2,* © 1977 c/o Elsevier), 25 ('Criteria of Corporate Social Performance' from D Boddy, *Management, an Introduction*, Pearson, Harlow 2007, pp.155–157), 31 mind map, 45/46 (information systems from D Boddy, *Management, an Introduction*, Pearson Harlow 2007, pp.383–387); Stefan Chabluk pp.4(figures 1.1, 1.2, 1.2), 60.

The publishers would like to thank the following for permission to use their photograph: Alamy Images p.22 (Business meeting/Yuri Arcurs).

Logos on page 16 by kind permission: BMW, Nokia, Proctor and Gamble, Nestle, Société des Products Nestlé S.A.